DATE DUE		

Vidor High School Library
Vidor, Texas 77662

ANTI-SEMITISM

Other Books in the At Issue Series:

ANTI-SEMITISM

Laura K. Egendorf, *Book Editor*

David Bender, *Publisher*
Bruno Leone, *Executive Editor*

Bonnie Szumski, *Editorial Director*
Brenda Stalcup, *Managing Editor*
Scott Barbour, *Senior Editor*

T 20048

An Opposing Viewpoints® Series

Greenhaven Press, Inc.
San Diego, California

Library of Congress Cataloging-in-Publication Data

Anti-Semitism / Laura K. Egendorf; book editor.
    p.   cm. — (At issue)
    Includes bibliographical references and index.
    ISBN 0-7377-0000-9 (pbk. : alk. paper). —
ISBN 0-7377-0001-7 (lib. : alk. paper)
    1. Anti-Semitism. 2. Christianity and anti-Semitism. 3. Afro-Americans—Relations with Jews. I. Egendorf, Laura K.,
    1973–   . II. Series: At issue (San Diego, Calif.)
    DS145.A599   1999
    305.892'4—dc21   98-11680
                                                                                               CIP

©1999 by Greenhaven Press, Inc., PO Box 289009,
San Diego, CA 92198-9009

Printed in the U.S.A.

Every effort has been made to trace owners of copyrighted material.

Table of Contents

Introduction

In Jewish theology, God deemed the Jews his "chosen people." Ironically, in their four-thousand-year history, Jews have frequently been chosen as a target for persecution by the societies in which they reside. Jews and the teachings of Judaism have almost always been seen as the "other"— whether as a monotheistic anomaly in pre-Christian times or as a suspiciously successful minority in the modern era, particularly in the largely Christian West. While violent anti-Semitism has mostly disappeared, many observers insist that anti-Semitism persists in less virulent forms. Although this anti-Semitism is not based wholly on theological disputes, examining the role of non-Jewish religions in fomenting anti-Jewish attitudes can deepen one's understanding of the nature and the extent of modern anti-Semitism. One religion that has played a key role in the spread and subsequent decline of anti-Semitism is Catholicism.

From its inception, the Catholic Church propagated anti-Jewish teachings. Christian theology taught that the Jews were infidels who had killed Jesus and rejected the true gospel. According to church doctrine, an essential requirement for Christian salvation was hatred of the Jews. Christianity also viewed Judaism as an obsolete religion that had been supplanted by the church and its Bible. Church policies in the Middle Ages separated Jews from the rest of the community, banned intermarriage, and imposed economic restrictions. Economic laws imposed by the church increased anti-Semitism; because Christians were not allowed to lend money at interest, while Jews were, Christians considered Jews to be evil usurers. Accusations of blood libel (claims that Jews killed Christian children and used their blood to make unleavened bread) developed out of Christian texts. The Crusades, incited by a speech by Pope Urban II in 1095, led to the massacre of thousands of "infidel" Jews.

In some ways, however, the Vatican was relatively friendly toward the Jews. According to Frederic Cople Jaher, a professor of history at the University of Illinois at Urbana-Champaign: "At the close of the Middle Ages, . . . Rome and the other papal territories alone afforded modest protection and privileges for Jews in western Europe." The Jews were never excluded from the Holy City, and the papacy's opposition to anti-Jewish violence made Rome and the rest of Italy a relatively safe place.

Although the Vatican may have opposed violence, the Inquisition provides an example of how Catholic teachings sometimes spread into deadly anti-Semitism. Pope Gregory IX formally established the papal Inquisition in 1233 in order to suppress heresy. The Inquisition did not formally target Jews, but in the middle of the thirteenth century, the Talmud was found to be blasphemous, and Inquisition tribunals censored and destroyed Jewish texts. Yet these actions were relatively mild compared to the Spanish Inquisition, which featured little involvement from the papacy. The Spanish Inquisitors tortured, executed, and ultimately expelled the nation's Jews and Marranos—Jews who had been forcibly baptized but were thought to secretly practice Judaism. Jews were expelled from various states throughout western Europe during the late Middle Ages, a time that was perhaps the worst period for European Jews until the 1930s and 1940s.

The Catholic Church and Judaism in the twentieth century

Anti-Semitism is inextricably linked with the Holocaust. The actions of Pius XII, the pope during that time, have been the source of much debate. Catholics, Jews, and others have argued over how many Jews he helped save and whether he could have, or should have, done more. While Pope Pius XII did write an encyclical in 1939 that condemned totalitarianism, the Vatican maintained formal relationships with Germany, and Pope Pius XII did not speak out against Nazi persecution of the Jews. Jonathan Tobin, a columnist for the *Jewish World Review*, writes, "The dominant tone of Pius's record during mankind's darkest hour was realpolitik rather than righteousness."

However, other people credit the pope with saving the lives of thousands of Jews, ordering them to be hidden within Vatican City and Rome. "Largely as a result of the church's efforts, Jews in Italy had a far higher survival rate under Nazi occupation than did those of other countries," George Sim Johnston asserts in the *New York Times*. Johnston cites the conversion of Chief Rabbi Israel Zolli to Catholicism after World War II as an indication of gratitude for what Pius XII had done for the Jews. Johnston and others argue that Jewish lives would have been in greater jeopardy had the pope been more vocal. The dispute over Pius XII's actions and whether the Catholic Church was complicit in the anti-Semitism of Nazi Germany would become a topic of international interest in the late 1990s.

While the events of World War II are still a matter of debate, as will be noted later, most analysts agree that since the mid-1960s, the Catholic Church has developed the most positive interfaith relationship with Judaism. Much of the credit for this improvement has been given to Pope John Paul II, but the changing attitude began with the 2nd Vatican Council, held between 1962 and 1965. The council's Declaration of Non-Christian Religions condemned anti-Semitism and stated that Jews cannot be blamed for Jesus's death.

Many people consider John Paul II's papacy, which began in 1978, as a time of unprecedented Catholic outreach toward Jews and a true indication of the Catholic Church's turning away from the anti-Semitism that marked its first two millennia. In 1985, the Vatican Commission for Religious Relations produced a document stating that Judaism is a living religion whose survival is desired and that Jewish fidelity to the Torah is to be admired, not seen as a stubborn refusal to accept Jesus's divinity. The commission also wrote that anti-Jewish passages in the Gospels should not be seen as truth but need to be understood within the historical context of the time they were written. Catholic textbooks and passion plays have been edited to eliminate anti-Semitic statements, especially as regards Jesus's death. In 1986, the pope was the first pontiff to visit a synagogue. The Vatican established diplomatic relationships with Israel in 1994. Many Jewish observers have praised these and similar actions. Tobin writes: "Where once the Church seemed to Jews to be the embodiment of hatred for Judaism and prejudice against the Jewish people, it now clearly stands among the righteous with its wholehearted condemnation of anti-Semitism."

Responses to the Holocaust

Despite the general goodwill of modern Catholicism toward Judaism, controversy has raged over the church's actions during the Holocaust. The debate began anew in March 1998, when the Vatican released a document, "We Remember: A Reflection on the *Shoah*," analyzing the role of the church during those years. While many people praised the document, others found it disappointing, especially in light of John Paul II's pro-Jewish actions.

The controversy centers over whether the document sufficiently acknowledges the church's role in the development of Nazism. While "We Remember" concedes that centuries of anti-Jewish teachings and Biblical interpretations resulted in discrimination, violence, expulsion, forced conversions, and other persecutions, the report states that Nazism was rooted in paganism, as opposed to Christian theology, and that the Nazis persecuted not just Judaism, but the church as well. Nazi anti-Semitism was rooted more in racism and nationalism than in religious differences, the document maintains. The work also expresses the regret of the Catholic Church that many Christians did not speak out against the Nazis: "At the end of this millennium the Catholic Church desires to express her deep sorrow for the failures of her sons and daughters in every age."

Critics argued that the Vatican commission did not offer an adequate apology or explanation for the Nazis' behavior and Pope Pius XII's response to it. An editorial in the *New Republic* criticized the Vatican commission for not acknowledging that Nazism's popularity was rooted in centuries of Christian anti-Semitism. Abraham H. Foxman, director of the Anti-Defamation League, an organization that fights anti-Semitism and hate crimes, asserted that the document rationalizes Pope Pius XII's failure to denounce the Nazis. Foxman and others contend that the Vatican paper paled in comparison to statements made by German and Polish bishops in January 1995, criticizing the behavior of some Christians during the Holocaust, and French bishops in October 1997, apologizing for the church's silence during the Holocaust. Some Christians agreed with these criticisms. An editorial in the Catholic magazine *Commonweal* maintains that while Pius XII did help many Jews and does not deserve condemnation, "We Remember" fails to acknowledge the church's culpability in the spread of anti-Semitism.

On the other hand, more conservative Catholic analysts praise the document. William Doino Jr. states in the *Wanderer*, a Catholic newspaper, that "We Remember" was not intended as an apology. He argues that Pope Pius XII was not silent during the Holocaust, noting that the document states that Jewish leaders and communities thanked the pontiff for all he had done. Doino also maintains that the church cannot be blamed for the sins of individual Catholics.

The debate over "We Remember" is an example of how much views of Jews and anti-Semitism have changed since the 1940s. The church's consistent repudiation of anti-Semitism in recent decades is, ironically, what led to the disappointment many felt over the document; had the document been written before John Paul II's papacy, many argue, it would have been more widely praised. The changing attitude of the Catholic Church is not unique; mainline Protestant denominations have also reevaluated their behavior. For the most part, blood libel and hatred of money-lending are seen as little more than medieval superstition. However, despite the many pro-Jewish strides made by the world's religions and most governments, debate continues over whether anti-Semitism persists in modern society. The evolution of Catholic views may be a model that others are attempting to emulate, or it may remain an anomaly. In *At Issue: Anti-Semitism*, the authors consider the prevalence and impact of anti-Semitism throughout the United States and the rest of the world.

1

Anti-Semitism Is an International Problem

Irwin Cotler

Irwin Cotler, a professor of law at McGill University in Montreal, is the former president of the Canadian Jewish Congress. He is on the board of directors of the International Centre for Human Rights and Democratic Development, an organization that supports the strengthening of human rights and democratic institutions.

Anti-Semitism is an international human rights issue, as exemplified by Holocaust denial and political rhetoric in Russia, the United States, and the Middle East. Anti-Semitism is also evident in criticisms of Israel's human rights record, particularly by the United Nations. Legal remedies, such as bringing Nazi war criminals to justice, are necessary to fight anti-Semitism.

Editor's note: The following viewpoint was originally a statement given to the House of Representatives Foreign Affairs Subcommittee on International Security, International Organizations and Human Rights on February 8, 1994.

We meet at a critical, historical juncture in the struggle for human rights and human dignity, in the relationship of anti-Semitism and human rights. A Dickensian universe, as described by Congress people, as being really the best of times and the worst of times. Where, on the one hand, there has been a literal explosion of human rights, where human rights has emerged as not only an organizing idiom of our political discourse, but of our political culture, to which, Mr. Chairman [Rep. Tom Lantos (D-CA)], you, have contributed so eloquently; where human rights has emerged, in a word, as the new secular religion of our time; where things thought and possible have not only happened, but have been forgotten, or are in danger of being forgotten, since the March of democracy from Central Asia to Central America, the dismantling of Apartheid, the repeal of the Zionism and racism resolution [a 1975 U.N. resolution equating Zionism with racism].

Reprinted from Irwin Cotler, statement submitted at the hearing "Global Dimensions of Anti-Semitism," before the House of Representatives Subcommittee on International Security, International Organizations, and Human Rights; Committee on Foreign Affairs; 103rd Cong., 2nd sess.; February 8, 1994.

And yet, at the same time, as statements have demonstrated, the violations in the world, the violations of human rights, continue unabated. The homeless of America, the hungry of Africa, the imprisoned of Asia, can be forgiven if they believe that somehow the human rights revolution has passed them by. While the silent tragedy of the Kurds, the ethnic cleansing in the Balkans, the horror of Sarajevo, the agony of Angola, Burundi, Sudan, are metaphor and message of the assault upon, indeed, abandonment of, human rights in our time.

The struggle against anti-Semitism must be seen not as a Jewish issue, but as a most profound justice issue.

What is true of the human condition generally in these violations of human rights? They find echo and expression in the graffiti of the Jewish condition, in the graffiti of anti-Semitism today. Where in the dialectics of Glasnost, the demons of the past, the repressed demons of the past racism and anti-Semitism, emerge once again, at the same time, the symbols of fascism, as Mr. Bronfman [Edgar Bronfman, president of World Jewish Congress] has stated, find rehabilitation. Where in the former Soviet Union, and in particular, in Russia, the new extremist nationalistic Russian right blames the Jews for bringing about communism, and the old extremist Communist left blames the Jews for the downfall of communism. Either way, the Jews are caught in a movement in the political uses of anti-Semitism in the former Soviet Union. Where coated, and not so coated, anti-Semitic discourse enters the mainstream of Western political discourse and popular culture. Examples have been given today, be it the race baiting, for example, of a David Duke, on the right, or a Louis Farrakhan, on the left. Where, in a word, this graffiti reflects and represents several generic trends respecting anti-Semitism and human rights, which for reasons of time, I will not enumerate, they are more elaborated in my paper itself.

Four trends in anti-Semitism

Number 1, the reoccurrence of this most enduring hatred, classical anti-Semitism, now finding its way into the popular culture and political discourse.

Two, the emergence of holocaust denial as the cutting edge of the new anti-Semitism. Feeding off the fascination with both Jews and conspiracies, and constituting, thereby, an assault, not only on the Jews in the killing of the Jews and their memory a second time, but an assault on human rights, in that this very holocaust denial movement, itself, constitutes an international conspiracy to cover up the worst Nazi crimes in history.

Third, a new anti-Semitism abroad in the land today, represented, in a word, in the ongoing de-legitimization of Israel and the Jewish people, reflected, if you will, in the emergence of Israel as the Jew among the nations, or with the Iranian Fatuah calling for the destruction of Israel as the Salmon Rushdie of the nations and extremist Islamic fundamentalists.

Four, the use of human rights, itself, as a cover under which this new anti-Semitism is carried out. In a word, in a world, as I began my statement, in which human rights is a secular religion of our time, Israel, portrayed as the poisoner of the international wells, as an anti-human rights metaphor, emerges as the new anti-Christ of our time.

And, finally, in the final dimension of this Orwellian dimension of the use of human rights as part of the assault, the use and abuse of the United Nations to give legitimation and sanction to the use and abuse of human rights as a cover for this new anti-Semitism. Ambassador Morris Abram, the Chair of the World Jewish Congress's U.N. watch, has given eloquent testimony to that, and it appears in my fuller statement.

The lessons of anti-Semitism

Finally, Mr. Chairman, may I conclude by way of summary with a number of one-liners, if you will permit me, respecting the relationship of anti-Semitism and human rights, both with respect of the lessons to be learned and the action to be taken. That is, history has shown that, while it may begin with Jews, it doesn't end with Jews. And so, the struggle against anti-Semitism must be seen not as a Jewish issue, but as a most profound justice issue.

That is, the Supreme Court of Canada put it, "The Holocaust did not begin in the gas chambers. It began with words, with racial incitement," a statement made by the Court in the course of upholding legal remedies to combat racial incitement. I have provided your committee with a statement respecting these legal remedies, which perhaps may be of some help here in the United States.

Nazism succeeded not only because of the pathology of hatred and the technology of terror, but because of the crime of indifference, because of the crime of silence. As Elie Wiesel put it, with echoes for Sarajevo today, neutrality always means coming down on the side of the victimizer, never on the side of the victim. It is our responsibility to shatter the walls of indifference to break these conspiracies of silence.

Bringing Nazi war criminals to justice, which Canada has done, is not only a profound issue of human rights, but also an antidote to the holocaust denial movement. In testimony before the courts in Canada, holocaust deniers have repeatedly said, "Well, you see. There have been no crimes. Therefore, there are no crimes. That must mean there are no so-called Nazi war criminals to be brought to justice."

And so, Mr. Chairman, if we do not persist in the bringing of Nazi war criminals to justice, there may be those who will say 10 or 15 years hence, "You see, there were no criminals. Therefore, that must mean that there were no crimes." The United Nations, founded, appropriately enough, as an alliance against racism and anti-Semitism must not be permitted to be converted into a forum for the propagation of racism and hatred itself.

May I close with these words? In a world which is not safe for democracy or human rights, it will not be safe for Jews, for Blacks, for any vulnerable minorities. The converse is also true, as history so tragically has shown, that in a world which will not be safe for Jews, and one could also now say for Blacks, Aboriginal, or any other visible minorities, it will not be safe for democracy or for human rights.

Anti-Semitism Has
Increased in the Middle East

Bernard Lewis

Bernard Lewis is Cleveland E. Dodge Professor of Near Eastern Studies Emeritus at Princeton University in Princeton, New Jersey. He is the recipient of the 1998 Ataturk International Peace Award, which is given to people who contribute to the development of world peace. Lewis is the author of many books, including The Shaping of the Modern Middle East *and* Semites and Anti-Semites: An Inquiry Into Conflict and Prejudice.

Anti-Semitism among Muslims has grown in recent years, due in part to negative reaction to the Israeli-Palestinian peace process. This Islamic anti-Semitism has European roots, such as belief in Jewish conspiracy theories and the popularity of texts such as *Protocols of the Elders of Zion*. Further aspects of this anti-Semitism are Holocaust denial, the banning or censoring of films that present positive portrayals of Jews, and textbooks that eliminate references to Jewish history. Despite the growing presence of Muslim anti-Semitism, the beginning of a dialogue between Arabs and Israelis has emerged.

What has come to be known as the peace process—the developing dialogue between the state of Israel on the one hand and the Palestinians and some Arab governments on the other—raised hopes that it would lead to a lessening of hostility and more specifically of anti-Semitism. In some quarters this did indeed occur. But in others the peace process itself has aroused a new Arab hostility to Jews, among both those frustrated by its slowness and those alarmed by its rapidity. As a result, anti-Semitism in recent years has conquered new territory and risen to a new intensity.

European anti-Semitism, in both its theological and racist versions, was essentially alien to Islamic traditions, culture, and modes of thought. But to an astonishing degree, the ideas, the literature, even the crudest inventions of the Nazis and their predecessors have been internalized and

Reprinted from Bernard Lewis, Afterword to the 2nd edition of *Semites and Antisemites* (London: Phoenix, 1997), ©1997 by Bernard Lewis, by permission of Orion Publishing Group Ltd.

Islamized. The major themes—poisoning the wells, the invented Talmud quotations, ritual murder, the hatred of mankind, the Masonic and other conspiracy theories, taking over the world—remain; but with an Islamic, even a Qur'anic twist.

The classical Islamic accusation, that the Old and New Testaments are superseded because Jews and Christians falsified the revelations vouchsafed to them, is given a new slant: the Bible in its present form is not authentic but a version distorted and corrupted by the Jews to show that they are God's chosen people and that Palestine belongs to them.[1] Various current news items—the scandal over Swiss banks accepting Nazi gold stolen from Jews, the appointment of Madeleine Albright as secretary of state, even the collapse of the Bank of Credit and Commerce International (BCCI)—are given an anti-Semitic slant. Jewish world plots—against mankind in general, against Islam, against the Arabs—have become commonplace.

The ideas, the literature, even the crudest inventions of the Nazis and their predecessors have been internalized and Islamized.

One of the crimes of Israel and of the Zionists in these writings is that they are a bridgehead or instrument of American or, more generally, of Western penetration. For such America is the Great Satan, Israel the Little Satan; Israel is dangerous as a spearhead of Western corruption. The more consistent European-type anti-Semites offer an alternative view; that America is the tool of Israel, rather than the reverse, an argument backed by a good deal of Nazi-style or original Nazi documentation. In much of the literature produced by the Islamic organizations, the enemy is no longer defined as the Israeli or the Zionist; he is simply the Jew, and his evil is innate and genetic, going back to remote antiquity. A preacher from Al-Azhar University explains in an Egyptian newspaper that he hates the Jews because they are the worst enemies of the Muslims and have no moral standards, but have chosen evil and villainy. He concludes: "I hate the Jews so as to earn a reward from God."[2]

The argument that "we cannot be anti-Semitic because we ourselves are Semites" may still occasionally be heard in Arab countries, though of course not in Turkey or Iran. But some of the more sophisticated spokesmen have become aware that to most outsiders this argument sounds silly or disingenuous. Some writers make a serious effort to maintain the distinction between hostility to Israel and Zionism and hostility to Jews as such. But not all. President Khatami of Iran, in his interview on CNN, pointed out—correctly—that "anti-Semitism is indeed a Western phenomenon. It has no precedents in Islam or in the East. Jews and Muslims have lived harmoniously together for centuries." A newspaper known to express the views of the "Supreme Guide" Khamenei rejected this statement as untrue: "The history of the beginnings of Islam is full of Jewish plots against the Prophet Muhammad and of murderous attacks by Jews . . . unequivocal verses in the Qur'an speak of the hatred and hostility of the Jewish people against Muslims. One must indeed distinguish between the Jews and the Zionist regime, but to speak in the manner we heard was exaggerated and there was no need for such a presentation."[3] The Egyptian director of a film about President Gamal Nasser reports a similar complaint by the late president's daughter. She objected to a passage in his film indicating that "Nasser was not against the Jews, but against Zionism, because she wanted to portray her father as a hero of the anti-Jewish struggle."[4]

Spokesmen of the government of Iran usually disclaim anti-Semitism; they refrain from overtly anti-Semitic phraseology and proclaim their readiness to tolerate Jews—of course within the limits prescribed by the *Shari'a* (Islamic law). This however does not prevent them from embracing the *Protocols of the Elders of Zion,* the hundred-year old Russian forgery alleging a Jewish plot to take over the world. These are frequently reprinted in Iran in book form and were even serialized in a daily newspaper "as a reminder to the reader."[5] Iranian networks also distribute copies of the *Protocols* internationally in various languages. In Egypt the *Protocols* formed the basis of an interview published in a popular Egyptian magazine with Patriarch Shenouda, head of the Coptic church.[6] The interviewer starts by introducing the *Protocols* as an authentic historical record and questions the patriarch, whose comments on Jews and Judaism seem to be based on the information supplied to him by the interviewer, and derived from the *Protocols* and another popular anti-Semitic forgery, the pseudo-Talmud.

Opposition to the peace process

Arab opposition to the peace process as such, or to the manner in which it is being conducted, is of three major types: political, economic, and Islamic.

The first is basically a continuance of what went before—ideological polemic against Zionism and political warfare against the state of Israel. Ideological or political opposition as such is not based on prejudice, but it affects and is affected by prejudice.

This kind of opposition and the prejudice associated with it continue to flourish and even to spread in spite of, and in some quarters because of, the peace process. It has been aggravated by some of the actions of the new Israeli government and still more by the utterances of some of its followers. Israeli extremists cannot really be blamed for the anti-Semitic propaganda in the Egyptian and other Arab media, which had already reached high levels of scurrility before the change of government and policy in Israel in June 1996; they have, however, undermined the efforts of well-meaning Arabs to counter these campaigns.

An example of reporting and comments on the news may be seen in reports of the suicide bombing in Ramat Gan on July 24, 1995. This act was disclaimed, even denounced, by responsible Palestinian and other Arab leaders. It was acclaimed by many others, from the center and the left as well as in the fundamentalist Islamic press. A leading article in a Jordanian leftist weekly by its editor, Fahd ar-Rimawi, acclaims the heroism of the Hamas bomber who "sent seven Zionist settlers to hell and thirty others to the casualty wards" and goes on to denounce those who had condemned the attack as hypocrites or worse.[7] That Ramat Gan is near Tel Aviv, part of Israel since the foundation of the state, makes the description of its inhabitants as "Zionist settlers" the more noteworthy. The Jordanian fundamentalist Ziyad Abu Ghanima rails against those who "shed torrents of tears in mourning for filthy Jewish blood while sparing their tears when Palestinian or Lebanese blood is shed by the hands of the Jews, may God curse them."[8]

More dangerous than this old-guard resistance is a new active opposition to the peace process that arises from the process itself, from a fear that the prowess which the Israelis had demonstrated in the battlefield would be equaled or even exceeded in activities with which Jews are more traditionally associated—in the factory, the counting house, and the marketplace. A certain Israeli brashness and lack of understanding of the courtesies and sensitivities of Middle Eastern society have often exacerbated such fears.

According to this perception, Israel has changed its tactics. It has now switched from warlike to peaceful methods to pursue its nefarious design of penetrating and dominating the Arab world. Some see dark menace in every Israeli attempt at communication and cooperation. The expansion of trade links means economic exploitation and subjugation; the development of cultural links means the subversion and destruction of Arab-Islamic culture; the quest for political relations is a prelude to imperial domination. These fantasies, absurd as they may seem to the outsider or indeed to any rational observer, nevertheless command wide support in the Arab media and particularly in Egypt.

For exponents of this view, European anti-Semitism provides a rich reservoir of themes and motifs, of literature and iconography, on which to draw and elaborate. Shimon Peres's book' *The New Middle East,*[9] with its somewhat idyllic view of future peaceful cooperation between Israel and the Arab states for economic improvement and cultural advancement, has appeared in several Arabic translations. The purpose of these translations is indicated in the blurb of one of them, published in Egypt:

> When the *Protocols of the Elders of Zion* were discovered about two hundred years ago [sic] by a Frenchwoman [sic] and disseminated in many languages including Arabic, the international Zionist establishment tried its best to deny the plan. They even claimed that it was fabricated and sought to acquire all the copies in the market in order to prevent them from being read. And now, it is precisely Shimon Peres who brings the decisive proof of their authenticity. His book confirms in so clear a way that it cannot be denied that the *Protocols* were true indeed. Peres's book is the last but one step in the execution of these dangerous designs.[10]

The *Protocols* remain a staple, not just of propaganda, but even of academic scholarship. Thus, according to an article in an Egyptian weekly,[11] the University of Alexandria accorded the degree of master of arts to the writer of an important "scientific treatise" dealing with the economic role of the Jews in Egypt in the first half of the twentieth century. The description of this dissertation makes it clear that its author relied very heavily on the *Protocols* and on the methodology of research that they provided.

A campaign attacking Israeli agricultural techniques and products—the one area in which there has been real cooperation with Egypt—accuses the Israelis of selling hormonally altered fruit that kills men's sperm. (They also supposedly supply Egyptian women with hyper-aphrodisiac chewing gum that drives them into a frenzy of sexual desire.) Other stories accuse the Israelis (or simply "the Jews") of supplying Egyptian farmers with poisoned seeds and disease-bearing poultry "like time bombs";[12] of deliberately spreading cancer among the Egyptians and other Arabs by devising and distributing carcinogenic cucumbers and shampoos; of promoting drug consumption and devil worship; and of organizing a campaign to legalize homosexuality to undermine Egyptian society. A Syrian paper even claims that Arafat made peace because he himself is a Jew.[13]

Islamic arguments

The strongest, most principled, and most sustained opposition to the peace process is offered in the name of Islam, especially by the government of Iran and its agencies, and by other Islamic parties and organizations. Islamic opposition has the considerable advantage of being ideologically formulated and logically consistent and of using familiar language to appeal to deep-rooted sentiments. This gives to arguments based on Islam far greater cogency and power than those based on nationality and race. Nevertheless, spokesmen for Islamic movements do not disdain to use racist arguments, and specifically, to draw on the rich resources of hatred provided by European anti-Semitism. Standard anti-Semitic themes have become commonplace in the propaganda of Arab Islamic movements like Hizbullah and Hamas, in the pronouncements of various agencies of the Islamic Republic of Iran, and even in the newspapers and other publications of Refah, the Turkish Islamic party whose head served as prime minister in 1996-97.

Most of these accusations are familiar and can be traced to their European sources. Others arise from local circumstances. Thus, for Turkish anti-Semites, the misdeeds of the Jews include the downfall of the Ottoman Empire and the recent troubles in Bosnia. In Iran, American sanctions and the resulting economic hardships are ascribed to sinister Jewish influences in Washington.

Other accusations are clearly transference or projection; for example, Israelis are allegedly told by rabbis that if they die while killing Palestinians they will go straight to paradise. Some are traditional Islamic accusations against the Jews, based on well-known passages in the Qur'an and *hadith* (sayings and actions attributed to the Prophet Muhammad). Some are borrowed or adapted from the standard armory of European anti-Semitism. Increasingly, the second and third motifs are combined.

Anti-Semitic propaganda

These different kinds of propaganda all share the technique of rewriting or obliterating the past, and in particular removing anything that might arouse compassion or evoke respect for the Jew. Standard themes include recasting ancient history, Holocaust denial, and equating Jews with Nazis.

Ancient history. The rewriting makes Jews disappear from the ancient Middle East. The historical museum in Amman tells through objects and inscriptions the history of all the ancient peoples of the region—with one exception. The kings and prophets of ancient Israel are entirely missing. I was able to find only three references to Jews. The first explains (in English) the inscription on the Mesha Stele as "thanking the Moabite god Chemosh for deliverance from the Israelites." (The Arabic explanation reads, "from the tyranny of the Israelites.") The second appears in an alcove containing the Dead Sea scrolls produced by a "Jewish sect." The third is a reference to "the militant Hasmonean Jews [who] . . . established their own reign in Palestine and the northern part of Jordan. Most of the Greek cities welcomed the Roman army headed by General Pompey as a liberator from Jewish oppression."

Textbooks used in schools under the Palestinian Authority lack even these few allusions to ancient Jewish history. For them, the history of Palestine begins with the retroactively Arabized Canaanites and jumps from them to the Arab conquest in the seventh century C.E., entirely omitting the Old Testament, its people and their history.

The strongest, most principled, and most sustained opposition to the peace process is offered in the name of Islam.

Holocaust denial. Either the Holocaust never happened, or if it did, it was on a small scale and—some add—the Jews brought it on themselves. Another favorite line is that the Zionists were the collaborators and successors of the Nazis. This remarkable version of history commands increasing Arab support, as is evidenced by the reception accorded to Roger Garaudy, a French ex-Communist convert to Islam who has published a book entitled *The Founding Myths of Israeli Politics.*[14] These myths are three: the religious myth of the Chosen People and the Promised Land; the Holocaust myth of Jewish extermination and Zionist anti-fascism, and the new myth of the modern Israeli miracle, actually due to foreign money procured by Jewish lobbyists. Garaudy's sources include apologists for Hitler, post-Zionist Israeli revisionists, and European anti-Americanists.

Garaudy's Middle East tour in the summer of 1996 was a triumph. In Lebanon he was received by the prime minister and the minister of education, in Syria by the vice president and several other ministers. He gave a number of highly publicized lectures and interviews in both countries and was welcomed by major literary and other intellectual bodies. In Jordan and Egypt he was not officially received but was welcomed with the same or greater acclaim in literary circles. The government-sponsored Arab Artists Union elected him an honorary member—the first since the Federation was established more than twenty years ago. The editor-in-chief of Egypt's semi-official *Al-Ahram* newspaper conferred a press prize on Garaudy in recognition of the "fresh air" that he had contributed to the debate. He was even invited to contribute a series of ten articles to an Arabic weekly published in London by BBC's Arabic service.[15]

Garaudy's welcome, however, was not unanimous. Some fundamentalists, while approving his views on Israel, questioned his understanding of Islam. In Morocco he was acclaimed by some newspapers, but his public appearances were canceled. "The universities," said the minister of higher education, "will not open their gates to anti-Semites."

Jews as Nazis. Denying or minimizing the Holocaust facilitates another favorite theme—that Jews, far from being victims of the Nazis, were their collaborators who now carry on their tradition. Cartoons depicting Israelis and other Jews with Nazi-style uniforms and swastikas have now become standard. These complement the Nazi-era hooked noses and blood-dripping jagged teeth. The memory of both the Jewish victims and Arab admirers of the Third Reich is totally effaced. To maintain this interpretation of history, some measure of control is necessary, extending even to entertainment. *Schindler's List,* a film portraying the suffering of the Jews under Nazi rule, is banned in Arab countries. Even *Independence Day,* which has nothing to do with either the Nazis or the Middle East, was denounced in Arab circles because it has a Jewish hero, and that is unacceptable. The film won approval for release in Lebanon only after the censors had removed all indications of the Jewishness of the hero—the skullcap, the Hebrew prayer, the momentary appearance of Israelis and Arabs working side by side in a desert outpost. A Hizbullah press liaison officer explained his objection to the film. "This film polishes and presents the Jews as a very humane people. You are releasing false images about them."[16]

While visits to Arab bookshops or to religious bookshops in Turkey reveal a wide range of anti-Semitic literature, any kind of corrective is lacking. The Arab reader seeking guidance on such topics as Jewish history, religion, thought, and literature will find virtually nothing available. Some material on modern Israel (e.g., that produced by the former Palestine Research Center in Beirut) is reasonably factual. But most of what is available is either lurid propaganda or used as such. Translations from Hebrew are few and fall mainly into three categories: accounts of Israeli espionage, memoirs by Israeli leaders (Rabin, Peres, Netanyahu), with explanatory introductions and annotations, and writings by anti-Zionist and anti-Israel Jews.

Hopeful signs

The peace treaties negotiated and signed between governments will remain cold and formal, amounting to little more than a cessation of hostilities, until peace is made between peoples. As long as a high-pitched scream of rage and hate remains the normal form of communication, such a peace is unlikely to make much progress.

But there are some signs of improvement, of the beginnings of a dialogue. Statesmen, soldiers and businessmen have been in touch with their Israeli opposite numbers, and some of these contacts have so far survived the change of government in Israel. Intellectuals have proved more recalcitrant, but even among them, there have been signs of change. A few courageous souls have braved the denunciation of their more obdurate colleagues to meet publicly with Israelis and even on rare occasions to visit Israel.

A number of Arab intellectuals have expressed disquiet and distaste with the vicious anti-Semitism that colors so much of the debate on the Arab-Israel conflict. The trial of Roger Garaudy in Paris in February 1998 for a violation of the Loi Gayssot, making Holocaust denial a criminal offense in France, evoked strong reactions in the Arab world. In general, there was an outpouring of vehement moral and substantial material support. But there were some dissenting voices. In the first of a number of articles condemning the cult of Garaudy, Hazim Saghiya drew attention to the contrast between Western and Arab criticisms of the trial in Paris. Western critics took their stand on freedom of expression, even for odious ideas. Arab critics, he observed, have in general shown little concern for freedom of expression; it was Garaudy's ideas that they liked.[17] Several other writers in the Arabic press expressed disapproval of the cult of Garaudy, and more generally, of Holocaust denial.

There were other hopeful signs. In January 1997 a group of Egyptians, Jordanians, and Palestinians, including intellectuals, lawyers, and businessmen, met with a similar group of Israelis in Copenhagen and agreed "to establish an international alliance for Arab-Israeli peace." Their declaration is not confined to pious generalities but goes into detailed discussion of some of the specific issues at stake. Needless to say, the Arab participants in this enterprise were denounced and reviled by many of their colleagues as dupes, traitors or worse.

A recent incident evoked disquieting memories of the rampage of the Egyptian gendarme Sulayman Khatir in 1985 when he shot at Israeli visitors, killing several and disabling nine of them. It also provided an encouraging contrast. On March 13, 1997, a Jordanian soldier, Ahmad Daqamsa, suddenly started firing at an Israeli girls' school outing, killing seven children and wounding several more before being overpowered by his comrades. In a gesture of contrition and compassion, King Husayn of Jordan a few days later crossed into Israel and called in person to offer his condolences to the bereaved families. Reactions in Jordan were mixed. Some of his people joined the Israelis in acclaiming this act of courage, human decency and generosity of spirit. Others, while condemning the murders, thought the king's response excessive. Others again made the murderer's home a place of pilgrimage. But there was nothing comparable with the outpouring of support that, for a while, made Sulayman Khatir a popular national and even intellectual hero in Egypt.

The Arab reader seeking guidance on such topics as Jewish history, religion, thought, and literature will find virtually nothing available.

Closer contact between the two societies may bring interesting, perhaps even valuable results. Israel with all its faults is an open, democratic society. A million Arabs are Israeli citizens; two million Palestinians have lived or are living under Israeli rule. Although this rule has often been harsh and arbitrary, by the standards of the region it has on the whole been benevolent. Two contrasting incidents illustrate a direction of possible change. During the *intifada,* a young Arab boy had his wrist broken by a baton-wielding Israeli soldier. He appeared next day, bandaged and in a hospital, denouncing Israeli oppression—on Israeli television. In 1997 a lawyer in Gaza submitted an article to a Palestinian journal describing the investigation by the Israeli police of the prime minister and other members of the Israeli government, and suggesting that similar procedures might be adopted by the Palestinian Authority. The editor of the journal did not publish the article but instead referred it to the attorney general who ordered the arrest and imprisonment of its author.

Growing numbers of Arabs see—and some even make this point. It did not pass unnoticed that the only public investigation of the Sabra and Shatila massacre was a judicial inquiry held in Israel. No such inquiry was held in any Arab country. The principal perpetrator of the massacre, Elie Hubayqa, a Lebanese Christian militia leader at that time allied with Israel, subsequently went over to the Syrian side and has for some years past been a respected member of the Syrian-sponsored government in Beirut. The election for the Palestinian Authority held in January 1996, acclaimed as the freest and fairest held in the Arab world, contrasted the more sharply with the show election held a little earlier in Lebanon in the presence of a different neighbor.

The Royal Institute for Interfaith Studies in Amman, under the patronage of Crown Prince Hasan, is concerned with Judaism as well as with Islam and Christianity. It has invited Jewish scholars from Israel and elsewhere to contribute to its activities and to its English-language journal.[18] This attempt to present Jewish beliefs and culture in objective terms, even to allow Jews to speak for themselves, is rare, and perhaps unique, in the Muslim world.

The last word may be left to 'Ali Salim, one of the first Egyptian intellectuals who dared to visit Israel. He said: "I found that the agreement between the Palestinians and the Israelis was a rare moment in history. A moment of mutual recognition. I exist and you also exist. Life is my right; it is also your right. This is a hard and long road. Its final stage is freedom and human rights. It will not be strewn with roses but beset with struggle and endurance. One cannot make peace just by talking about it. There is no way to go but forward, to achieve peace with deeds and not just words."[19]

Notes

1. *Ash-Sha'b*, Jan. 3, 1997; *Al-Watan* (Muscat), Feb. 12, 1997.

2. *Al-Ittihad*, Dec. 20, 1996.

3. *Jumhuri-i Islami*, Jan. 8, 1998.

4. *La Presse de Tunisie*, Jan. 26, 1998.

5. *Ettela'at* published the *Protocols* in 1995 in more than 150 installments.

6. *Al-Musawwar*, Dec. 27, 1996.

7. *Al-Majd*, July 31, 1995.

8. *Shihan*, July 29, 1995.

9. Shimon Peres with Arye Naor, *The New Middle East* (New York: Henry Holt, 1993).

10. Muhamad Hilmi 'Abd al-Hafiz, trans., *Ash-Sharq al-Awsat al-Jadid* (Alexandria: n.p., 1995).

11. *Akhir Sa'a.* Dec. 25, 1996.

12. *Ash-Sha'b* (Cairo), Mar. 14, 1997.

13. *Ath-Thawra*, Oct. 4, 1995.

14. *Les mythes fondateurs de la politique israelienne* (Paris: Samizdat, 1996).

15. *Al-Mushahid as-Siyasi*, May 4, 11, 18, 25; Jun. 1, 8, 15, 22, 29; July 6, 1997.

16. *Al-'Ahd*, Nov. 15, 1996

17. *Al-Hayat*, Jan. 15, 1998.

18. *Interfaith Newsletter*, Mar.–Sept. 1995; *Interfaith Monthly*, Sept. 1995.

19. 'Ali Salim, *Rihla ila Isra'il*, (Cairo: Akhbar al-Yawm, 1994), p. 8.

3

The Christian Right Is Anti-Semitic

Skipp Porteous

Skipp Porteous is the publisher of Freedom Writer, *a newsletter published by the Institute for First Amendment Studies (IFAS), an educational and research organization that focuses on church-state issues. He is the author of* Jesus Doesn't Live Here Anymore: From Fundamentalist to Freedom Writer.

The Christian Right is the source of much anti-Semitism. Examples of Christian Right anti-Semitism include stereotypes of Jewish behavior and appearance, missionary activities, Christian homeschool textbooks, and the Christian Identity Movement. Attacks on Jews are also disguised as attacks on humanism, an approach taken by Tim LaHaye and Donald Wildmon, among others.

A study by the Institute for First Amendment Studies found a prevalence of anti-Semitism within the Christian Right. While some of the prejudice and hostility toward Jews is concealed, much is blatant. Stereotyping of Jews is widespread; and anti-Semitism in the form of aggressive missionary activity threatens the very existence of Judaism.

Several disturbing trends indicate that—unless sweeping changes are made—anti-Semitism within conservative Christianity will not only continue as a long-term problem, but will escalate sharply. Thousands of private Christian schools and Christian home schools utilize anti-Semitic textbooks. These textbooks include the "original" McGuffey's Readers, which have enjoyed a tremendous resurgence in recent years, and books published by Bob Jones University Press for use in Christian schools.

Additionally, the Christian Right's anti-abortion movement has anti-Semitic overtones. Anti-abortion groups such as Operation Rescue and Life Dynamics list "Jewish doctors" as the leading performers of abortion.

So-called "humanism" is under attack by the Religious Right in schools and other institutions across the country. Condemnation of humanism has anti-Semitic roots. Though seldom mentioned, Christian Right leaders link humanism with Judaism, saying "Judaism grew out of

Reprinted from Skipp Porteous, "Anti-Semitism: Its Prevalence Within the Christian Right," *Freedom Writer*, May 1994, by permission of the author.

the rejection of Jesus Christ and steadily became humanism."[1]

Other disturbing observations involve a melding of extreme right-wing anti-Semites and their mainstream counterparts. Pastor Pete Peters, a nationally known anti-Semitic Christian Identity preacher, has found a home on the Keystone Inspiration Network. This Christian "family" network is available on cable TV in approximately 120 cities across the country.

The Rev. Donald Wildmon, the Methodist minister who heads the American Family Association (AFA), is no stranger to accusations of anti-Semitism. Though he denies being anti-Semitic, he has emerged as the darling of the anti-Semitic Liberty Lobby. In fact, his AFA has a special spot on Liberty Lobby's LogoPlex, an extreme-rightist computer bulletin board service.

Two forms of anti-Semitism

Ofttimes, only the most blatant anti-Semitic incidents are reported. Much of the anti-Semitism within conservative Christianity goes unnoticed and unreported. Some forms are so subtle that only those familiar with the code words and innuendo can spot it.

Stereotyping is among the most common form of anti-Semitism. This is evidenced by the words of many well-known Christian leaders, among them the Rev. Bailey Smith. "I don't know why God chose the Jew," Smith said. "They have such funny noses."[2]

Outward appearance, though, is not the only way some leaders characterize Jews. The Rev. Dan C. Fore, former head of the Moral Majority in New York, said, "I love the Jewish people deeply. God has given them talents He has not given others. They are His chosen people. Jews have a God-given ability to make money. . . . They control the media, they control this city."[3]

"A few of you don't like the Jews and I know why," said the Rev. Jerry Falwell. "He [sic] can make more money accidently than you can make on purpose."[4]

A second form of anti-Semitism involves missionary activity directed at Jews. Many conservative Christian leaders hold the view that Judaism is an invalid religion, that Jews who don't believe in Jesus are "unsaved" or "incomplete." The offensiveness of this type of anti-Semitism should be obvious, but often goes unnoticed.

"It's interesting at great political rallies," preached the Rev. Bailey Smith, "how you have a Protestant to pray, a Catholic to pray, and then you have a Jew to pray. With all due respect to those dear people, my friends, God Almighty does not hear the prayer of a Jew. For how in the world can God hear the prayer of a man who says that Jesus Christ is not the true Messiah? That is blasphemy."[5]

The Rev. Jerry Falwell sanctioned this viewpoint in his book, *Listen, America!* "The Jews are returning to their land of unbelief. They are spiritually blind and desperately in need of their Messiah and Savior. Yet they are God's people, and in the world today Bible-believing Christians are the best friends the nation Israel has."[6]

Falwell correctly points out that he and other American fundamentalist Christians support the nation of Israel. It should be noted, however, that this support is for a piece of real estate, the land of Israel, and not necessarily for the Jewish people.

Pat Robertson, too, thinks of Jews as "spiritually deaf" and "spiritually blind." In the end times, Robertson believes, Jews will be brought in as "offerings to the Lord."[7] He predicts mass conversions of Jews to Christianity, and toward this end, Robertson built a Christian radio station in Lebanon to beam the Gospel into the Jewish state, which Fundamentalists believe will eventually be inherited by Christians. For the present, Jews occupy the land as caretakers.

Many Christian organizations presume an obligation to convert Jews to Christianity. While Jews for Jesus may be the most well-known of these groups, according to Mark Powers, national director of Jews for Judaism, more than 450 missionary organizations specifically target Jews in the United States, Canada, and Israel. More than 350,000 American Christians now identify themselves as former Jews; 140,000 of that total call themselves "Hebrew Christians."

One group, the Christian Jew Foundation (CJF), publishes a newsletter called *The Message of the Christian Jew*. An ugly article by Charles Halff, the group's executive director, titled "The Blindness of the Jew"[8] stated:

"Gentile Christians sometimes wonder why Jewish evangelism is such difficult and discouraging work. Our missionaries are spat on, ridiculed, threatened, maligned, and sometimes physically abused.

"David Zauber, our CJF missionary in Georgia, is a Jewish Christian—and weighs probably 150 pounds, soaking wet! He was passing out Gospel tracts near the subway a few years ago, when a Jewish man knocked him down with his fist. By the time David caught his breath and got back to his feet, the man had disappeared into the crowd. This is just one example of the difficulties our missionaries face.

"We wonder, why are the sons of Israel so belligerent and hard-hearted?"

Halff answered his rhetorical question. "As we look at Jews today, we see that they are blinded by tradition; they are blinded by prejudice; and they are blinded by self-righteousness." He adds, "The majority of them live by the Talmud, rather than by the Old Testament. Judaism is a religion of works and tradition. One such tradition is the practice of waving a chicken overhead and chanting, 'This is my sacrifice!' We know this is absolutely contrary to the teaching of the New Testament, since the blood of Messiah (Jesus) had been shed for the sins of many, and 'there is no more offering for sin' (Hebrews 10:18.)"

Much of the anti-Semitism within conservative Christianity goes unnoticed and unreported.

One entire issue of *The Message of the Christian Jew*[9] dealt with anti-Semitism. While acknowledging the most overt types of anti-Semitism, the writers failed to see how Christian missionary activity is a threat to the very existence of Judaism. In fact, an article by Gary Hedrick, the group's president, utilized a strange approach.

"Let us not forget, however," Hedrick wrote, "that a more subtle form of anti-Semitism is now sweeping our land. It's known by a variety of names, but most notably as the 'Two-Covenant,' or 'Dual-Covenant' movement. Its proponents claim that the Jewish people have their own Sinai Covenant and therefore have no need of the Gospel of Jesus Christ.

"Can you think of a more diabolical form of anti-Semitism than the view that the Gospel of Jesus Christ is for Gentiles, but not for Jews?"

Anti-Semitism and Christian schools

With an estimated 500,000 children being taught at home, the home school movement is a rapidly growing phenomena. *Newsweek's* Sam Allis called Christian Fundamentalism "the backbone of the home-school movement." One series of books, McGuffey's Eclectic Readers, popular with both Christian schools and home schools, influence the minds of tens-of-thousands of impressionable youngsters.

These are the same books originally published in 1836 by the Rev. William H. McGuffey. With 19th century sales of 125 million copies, McGuffey is considered "the author of the most popular schoolbook ever written." McGuffey's original Readers were, according to the current publishers, "Christ-centered." In time, though, most of the religious references were removed.

McGuffey's original Readers, now reborn for use in Christian homes and schools, are sexist, racist, and anti-Semitic. While the Readers reflect the time in which they were written, their use today indicates a giant step backward in human relations. The sexist aspects of the Readers promote "proper" roles for men and women. Among the racism portrayed is the constant referral to Native Americans as "savages." The anti-Semitism found in the McGuffey's Readers takes several forms.

A line from the Eclectic Third Reader warns students about the perils of rejecting Christianity. "It will cost something to be a Christian: it will cost more not to be so."[10]

In the same Reader, Christianity is championed as the only dependable religion. "There are no principles but those of CHRISTIANITY, to be depended upon in cases of REAL DISTRESS." (Emphasis in original)[11]

Jewish veneration of the Scriptures is denigrated. "The Old Testament has been preserved by the Jews in every age, with a scrupulous jealousy, and with a veneration for its words and letters, bordering on superstition . . ."[12]

McGuffey suggests that the rise of Christianity was not only predicted in the Old Testament, but was a result of Jewish infidelity toward God—a common anti-Semitic theme. The Reader mentions ". . . the Jews as the keepers of the Old Testament." Then, "It was their own sacred volume, which contained the most extraordinary predictions concerning the infidelity of their nation, and the rise, progress, and extensive prevalence of Christianity."[13]

In one fell swoop, McGuffey obliterates Jewish moral law, and all other moral teachings before Jesus. "The morality taught by Jesus Christ was purer, sounder, sublimer, and more perfect than had ever before entered into the imagination, or proceeded from the lips of man."[14]

In Lesson XVIII, dealing with Divine inspiration of the Gospel, the Eclectic Fourth Reader asks, "Why is it inconceivable that the book is fiction?" The answer, "The Jewish authors were incapable of the diction, and strangers to the morality, contained in the gospel . . ."[15]

A short story called "The Blind Preacher," recounts a blind minister's sermon about the trial and crucifixion of Jesus. The story reinforces the notion that Jews are responsible for the death of Jesus. "We saw the very faces of the Jews, the staring, frightful distortions of malice and rage."[16]

In fact, every single reference to Jews in McGuffey's Readers is negative. No effort is made to explain Judaism, or to teach what Jews believe.

The McGuffey Readers series is frequently advertised by the Conservative Book Club on the back of the Rev. Donald Wildmon's magazine, the *AFA Journal*, and in Pat Robertson's *Christian American*. The ads proclaim: "The ORIGINAL McGuffey's Readers were different. They were Christian." Copy in the ad says, ". . . give them some of the memorable poetry and prose of our Anglo-American inheritance . . ."

Two companies, Mott Media, of Milford, Michigan, and Thoburn Press, of Tyler, Texas, publish the "original" McGuffey's Eclectic Readers. The seven-volume set has been reprinted from the originals.

Several organizations that provide textbooks to Christian home schoolers promote the use of McGuffey's Readers. One, Christian Liberty Academy Satellite Schools (CLASS), now publishes its own Eclectic Reader. Michael McHugh, curriculum administrator for CLASS, reported that his organization sold between 5,000 and 6,000 of the Thoburn McGuffey's Readers to home schools.

Since 1982, Mott Media has sold a whopping 100,000 sets of the Readers. "Last year [1993] we started our Home School Book Club," Joyce Bowen, Mott Media's general manager, said. "In less than a year we sold between 4,000 and 5,000 sets to home schools."

The widespread use of McGuffey's Readers is a good indication of what children are being taught about Jews in many Christian schools and home schools. With the rapid growth of these schools, this should be of concern to caring Christian parents and responsible Christian leaders.

In other Christian textbooks, anti-Semitism exists by omission. The curriculum used by many Christian schools neglects Jewish accomplishments and positive contributions to history. This is documented by Albert J. Menendez in *Visions of Reality: What Fundamentalist Schools Teach*, a report on the textbooks used in Christian Fundamentalist schools:

McGuffey's original Readers, now reborn for use in Christian homes and schools, are sexist, racist, and anti-Semitic.

"Surprisingly, Jews and Judaism are almost invisible in these volumes. No mention is made of any Jewish contribution to U.S. history nor are any Jewish personalities in literature, sports or the arts mentioned. There is no reference to justices Frankfurter, Brandeis or Cardozo. The only Jews mentioned are Karl Marx, who is called 'an atheistic German Jew,'[17] and Sigmund Freud. It is noted that Jews were persecuted in Catholic countries but nothing is said about anti-Jewish discrimination in Protestant countries. Jewish supporters of Columbus are mentioned, as is the suggestion that Columbus may have been seeking a refuge for Jews.

"One passage in a world history text, however, blames Jews for the crucifixion of Jesus. 'The Jewish religious leaders, whose blindness and hypocrisy Jesus had denounced, sought to put Him to death. They brought Christ before the Roman governor Pontius Pilate, charging that Christ had disrupted the state. . . . Although Pilate found no fault in Jesus, he desired to maintain the peace. Giving in to the Jewish demands, he sentenced Jesus to death by crucifixion.'[18] In addition, we are informed, 'God used the destruction of Jerusalem to separate the early church from its Jewish environment and to scatter Christians throughout the Roman Empire.'[19]

"And one strange passage in a biology text says, 'The Jews were pruned for the Gentiles' sake, but they were also pruned for their disbelief.'"[20]

Anti-Semitism and anti-abortion

There are indications that the Christian Right's anti-abortion crusade has anti-Semitic components. In 1989, *Newsweek* magazine reported that Randall Terry, founder of the anti-abortion group Operation Rescue, said, "We have tried to do some outreach to the black and Jewish communities," but admitted that those efforts have failed, ". . . and that he is critical of the Jewish doctors, who he believes perform a large number of abortions."[21]

In doing research for this report, Operation Rescue National referred us to Life Dynamics Incorporated, a Christian anti-abortion organization based in Dallas, for specific information on abortion. Life Dynamics is an important research arm of the Christian Right's anti-abortion crusade. According to Life Dynamics, 26% of all doctors who perform abortions are Jewish (A spokesperson for Planned Parenthood called this figure "ludicrous.") Considering that Jews comprise only 2% of the population, this figure is disproportionately high.

The thought is not lost in Life Dynamics' popular *Bottom Feeder* "joke book." *Bottom Feeder* is an assortment of hackneyed jokes aimed at doctors who perform abortions. The jokes and cartoons are crude, scatological, and suggest that abortionists have sex with animals. Significantly, *Bottom Feeder* contains a number of references to Jews, and consistently portrays in cartoon form doctors who perform abortions as having exceptionally large noses, an age-old anti-Semitic allusion to Jews.

Examples of *Bottom Feeder*'s references to Jews include a list of the "four shortest books in the world." One is entitled "Famous Jewish Astronauts." One joke favors Adolf Hitler over an abortionist. It goes, "Q. What would you do if you found yourself in a room with Hitler, Mussolini and an abortionist, and you had a gun with only two bullets? A. Shoot the abortionist twice."

Aware that a high percentage of Jews are liberal and pro-choice, the anti-abortion movement targets Jews as "baby killers."

Additionally, a considerable number of the people involved in groups such as Operation Rescue, Lambs of Christ, and Missionaries to the Preborn, teach their children at home, using McGuffey's Readers and other materials mentioned in the section on Christian schools and home schools.

The Christian Right anti-abortion movement often refers to abortion as "the Holocaust in America." [Newsweek, May 1, 1989] This phrase is notable only for its shock value. To even remotely equate the two, especially in such a cavalier manner, offends not only Jews, but everyone who is aware of the horrors of the Nazis. Rabbi Balfour Brickner, Rabbi Emeritus of the Stephen Wise Free Synagogue in New York, said, "The Holocaust stands alone. . . . There are no legitimate or acceptable analogies."

Anti-Semitism and humanism

For years, anti-Semitic innuendo has cleverly passed as simply an attack on humanism. By employing a sort of "bait and switch" tactic, the conservative Christian right has shifted all the blame for the world's ills from the Jews to "humanists"—whom conservatives suspect are mostly Jews anyway. The theory here is that humanism is a "secular religion" that evolved out of modern Judaism. Instead of saying that Jews control the financial institutions, the media, the entertainment industry, and education, it is now the humanists who are in control.

This is borne out in the teachings of Rousas John (R.J.) Rushdoony, a former Presbyterian minister who is known as the "father of Christian Reconstruction." While Rushdoony is not well-known outside the circle of conservative Christian leadership, his influence within the movement is substantial. Rushdoony is a prolific author and his books approach bestseller status, shaping contemporary Christian thought since the 1960s. Rushdoony, a profound Christian thinker, is never afraid to say what some other Christian leaders are merely thinking.

According to Gary North, Rushdoony's son-in-law, "Rushdoony identified the underlying problem a generation ago: 'JUDAISM grew out of the rejection of Jesus Christ and STEADILY BECAME HUMANISM [emphasis added], and the Talmud is essentially the exposition of humanism under the facade of Scripture.'"[22]

Judaism became humanism! To grasp this concept is to understand why some notable Christian leaders exhibit hostility toward humanists. Leaders of the radical Christian Right know that many influential Jewish leaders are wholly secular. That is, they embrace Jewish culture, without observing the rituals of Judaism.

Another Christian writer is the Rev. Tim LaHaye, former leader of the Moral Majority. LaHaye is married to Beverly LaHaye, head of the 600,000-member Concerned Women for America organization.

In his 1980 book, *The Battle for the Mind*, LaHaye unleashed a vicious attack against humanism. Jews have traditionally been accused of everything for which LaHaye blames humanists. Our country is ". . . controlled by a small but very influential cadre of committed humanists . . ."[23] Pornography is the fault of "the humanist controllers of the American Civil Liberties Union and their humanist partners in moral crime—the judges who were appointed by the humanist politicians."[24]

"When the humanists came to America, their obstacles seemed overwhelming. But rather than waste their resources, they concentrated on using four vehicles to penetrate the minds and lives of our people: education, the media, organizations, and government."[25]

"We have already seen how John Dewey and his fellow humanists took over education . . ."[26] While Dewey wasn't Jewish, many of his colleagues were.

"Space does not permit a detailed account of how newspapers from coast to coast were gradually purchased by powerful, monied interests. As radio came into view, it was bought up by some of these same interests. Later, when TV licenses became available, the humanists flooded the field. Today, it is all humanistically controlled."[27]

"This news is carefully edited before being sent out to the daily papers. Who does the editing? Who hired the editors, and what are their beliefs? Anyone really familiar with humanism can recognize its influence in the way the news is managed."[28]

"It is obvious, by the degenerate programming that has appeared in recent years, that the three major networks (ABC, NBC, and CBS) are predominantly controlled by amoral humanists."[29]

"Not all the fifty or so people who control network news are committed humanists, but most of them are."[30]

"The humanists see TV as a vehicle, first, to indoctrinate and second, to make money. Shortly after learning that Norman Lear was the producer of the most amoral 'comedy' series on TV (such as the infamous Mary Hartman, Mary Hartman), I had lunch with a Christian businessman who told me how relieved he was to have sold his cable TV stations. Guess who bought them? Norman Lear."[31]

"There is one easy way to illustrate whose team Hollywood has really been on during the last fifty years. They rarely make a film that shows Communism as a world aggressor or murderer of the people—particularly of their own. Anti-German and anti-Japanese films abound . . ."[32]

"Sixty years of Communist crime against humanity provide ample material to draw on, but not if you're afraid to show humanistic socialism in a bad light."[33]

Why, in LaHaye's opinion, are humanists "soft" on Communism? It is entirely possible, if not probable, that the Rev. LaHaye equates Socialist/Communist Jews with Humanists. In many instances, the words are interchangeable.

In "A Special Jewish History Issue" of *The Truth At Last*,[34] a tabloid published by Dr. E.R. Fields in Marietta, Georgia, the assertion is made that "the original founders of Communism were all Jews." The author names Lenin as "a secret Jew." Furthermore, the article states that these Communist Jews came to America and established "the U.S. Communist Party and other socialist groups." This echoes LaHaye's theories on "humanists" coming to America to establish socialist groups, armed with a plan to penetrate and control the minds of the American people.

Oftentimes, conservatives' use of "humanism," "socialism," "communism," and "Jews" are interchangeable. Of course, "humanism" is a more palatable word when speaking to the general public.

The anti-Semitism of Christian ministers

"The American Ethical Union, founded in 1889 in New York City, was a federation of over thirty ethical societies that had been initiated by Felix Adler (Jewish) more than a decade earlier. New York became the capital of the humanist movement, which then spread across the United States."[35]

It is common knowledge that there are more Jews in New York than in any other city in the United States. (On extremist computer bulletin boards, New York is often referred to as "Jew York City.") It is well-known that many Jews who wanted to retain Jewish ethics, without the religious observances, led the Ethical Culture movement.

LaHaye considers the American Civil Liberties Union, headed by Ira Glasser and Nadine Strossen (both Jewish), "The most effective humanist organization for destroying the laws, morals, and traditional rights of Americans." LaHaye adds, "The anti-Christian attitude of the ACLU is not only evident in its persistent attack on moral legislation but also in its efforts to compel our country to become totally secular."[36]

LaHaye refers to "humanist attorney" William Kuntsler (Jewish) as "Communist oriented." He then attacks the Humanist Manifesto II, which like the original Humanist Manifesto, "criticizes religious dogmatism and denies the existence of a Creator."

Dr. Tim Madigan is the editor of the humanist magazine *Free Inquiry*. His publisher, Dr. Paul Kurtz, drafted the Humanist Manifesto II, which LaHaye so despises. Madigan said that he thinks about a third of the signers of Humanist Manifesto II were Jewish.

The Rev. Tim LaHaye's crusade against humanism parallels almost every anti-Semitic movement in recent history. In fact, Jews do have considerable influence in some of the arenas LaHaye writes about. Are these similarities coincidental, or is the campaign against humanism—attributing society's every evil to supposed humanists—really a covert attack on Jews?

The curriculum used by many Christian schools neglects Jewish accomplishments and positive contributions to history.

LaHaye is not the only conservative Christian minister whose assault on humanism raises serious questions about anti-Semitism.

The Rev. Donald Wildmon, founder and head of the American Family Association (formerly the National Federation for Decency) has, by design or chance, espoused Rushdoony's idea that modern Judaism is really humanism. With Wildmon, it is sometimes difficult to tell what group he's attacking—humanists or Jews. It appears that in his mind they are one and the same.

In Wildmon's view, television network executives (a majority of whom are Jewish, according to a Lichter-Rothman survey he often quotes) are in a deliberate conspiracy to promote "anti-Christian" television programming to undermine Christianity.

Wildmon made his first anti-Semitic innuendo before a convention of the National Religious Broadcasters (NRB) in 1985. And as early as 1981, Wildmon said, "Most television producers are of the Jewish perspective."[37]

The Anti-Defamation League (ADL) of B'nai B'rith wrote to Wildmon after a number of NRB attenders expressed concern about his presentation. "Your remarks imply that Jews create and condone anti-Christian programming," the ADL wrote on June 18, 1985. "You seem to be saying that the fact that there are so many Jews involved with commercial television programming is an explanation for the anti-Christian nature, as you see it, of that programming." Wildmon ignored the ADL's letter.

In 1985, Wildmon wrote a book called *The Home Invaders*, published by Victor Books, of Wheaton, Illinois. Anti-Semitic aspersion is carefully woven into the book.

In one section, Wildmon states, "Only a relatively small handful of people determine what Americans can and will see on network television. These people are overtly hostile to the Christian faith."[38]

He doesn't say who "these people" are until the next chapter. Wildmon's modus operandi is to quote someone else and then add his interpretation. In this case, he made use of a remark by columnist Pat Buchanan: "If he [playwright Christopher Durang] were as anti-Semitic as he is anti-Christian, he would neither be collecting awards nor staging any more plays."

Wildmon's interpretation of Buchanan's statement: "Buchanan is no doubt referring to the fact that Hollywood and the theater world is heavily influenced by Jewish people."[39]

In his *NFD Journal*,[40] Wildmon again raised the specter of a conspiracy among network executives (stating that 59% of them are Jewish) to create prime time "anti-Christian" programming. Wildmon concluded, "What we are witnessing by the networks and advertisers is a genuine hostility towards Christians and the Christian faith. This anti-Christian programming is intentional and by design. It took me years to believe that, and to be willing to say so publicly, but it is true."[41]

Time and time again, in his *AFA Journal* (formerly known as the *NFD Journal*), Wildmon has used the same inflammatory rhetoric.

On October 27, 1987, Wildmon wrote a letter to major television advertisers demanding that they stop advertising on shows that had an "anti-Christian" bias. Using the Lichter-Rothman study, he again blamed Jews for this objectionable programming.

Reactions to Donald Wildmon

Stuart Lewengrub, director of the ADL's southeast regional office, in a letter[42] to Robert L. Brannon, then vice president of the Holiday Corporation, wrote: "ADL initially sought to communicate with him [Wildmon] in a low key, non-accusatory, manner. I've enclosed a copy of a letter ADL sent Wildmon when he first began to employ the anti-Semitic innuendo. We were trying to give him the benefit of the doubt, at least insofar as his singling out the Jewish background of those 'anti-Christian' media folks was concerned. It is evident that he has little desire to alter that approach . . ."

He continues, "Based on what I understand about Wildmon, he tries to evade the 'anti-Semitism' issue by noting that the study on which he based his statistics was conducted by Jews (the Lichters and Rothman), which is true, but irrelevant to Wildmon's use of those statistics."

Lewengrub concluded, "One final thought—I am reminded of one of the most poignant comments to emerge from the Nazi Holocaust. You recall the scenes in pre-war Germany of thousands of people hurling 'unwanted' books into huge bonfires. It was said that 'A NATION THAT BURNS ITS BOOKS WILL SOON BURN ITS PEOPLE.' Prophetic, but I doubt Wildmon would understand or care."

S. Robert Lichter, a co-author of the Lichter-Rothman report, in a letter[43] to Brannon, said that his survey ". . . drew no conclusions about the nature of [TV] programming or the precise motivations of program directors." He also said, ". . . we naturally abhor any imputation of anti-Semitic inferences from our survey of television producers and executives."

Stanley Rothman, the other co-author of the Lichter-Rothman report, wrote[44] directly to Rev. Wildmon. Rothman strongly repudiated Wildmon's use of the Lichter-Rothman study to prove that Jewish producers are anti-Christian. Rothman stated: "The inferences you draw from our data are not justified." Rothman told Wildmon that their findings presented 'NO EVIDENCE' to support any of Wildmon's accusations, and that a new study actually proved the contrary. Wildmon ignored Rothman's letter and continued perpetrating this misinformation.

Oftentimes, conservatives' use of "humanism," "socialism," "communism," and "Jews" are interchangeable.

Harry E. Moore, Jr., regional director (Memphis), of the National Conference of Christians and Jews, in a letter[45] to Brannon, referred to Wildmon's alleged anti-Semitism. Moore said, "I agree that whether he [Wildmon] intends it or not, there is a not so subtle strain of anti-Semitism in his madness." He concluded, "I shall keep a wary eye on Mr. Wildmon. There is no telling which way his anti-Semitic bias will lead him."

In the fall of 1988, Robert K. Lifton, president of the American Jewish Congress, in a letter to prospective members, wrote, ". . . when Right Wing Christians launched their unsuccessful campaign to block release by Universal Studios of "The Last Temptation of Christ," they picked a very special target. THEY WENT AFTER THE JEWS."

"The Reverend Donald Wildmon, Executive Director of the American Family Association of Tupelo, Mississippi, mailed 500,000 letters [according to Wildmon, the final total was about 4 million letters] urging recipients to bring pressure upon "THE NON-CHRISTIAN OFFICIALS WHO RUN UNIVERSAL." Lifton added, "To be sure, films on such sensitive issues are bound to upset some people, and the right to criticize them is a constitutional right that we at the AJ Congress will defend. But, as we pointed out forcefully to these fundamentalists leaders, the exercise of this constitutional right 'DOES NOT CREATE LICENSE TO ENGAGE IN BIGOTRY AND ANTI-SEMITISM."

In the *AFA Journal*,[46] Rev. Wildmon quoted a Jewish colleague, Judith Reisman, who had come to his defense against charges of anti-Semitism. Reisman's words amplify Rev. Wildmon's alleged bigotry. She said, "The statements Rev. Wildmon has made which have been misconstrued as anti-Semitic, refer instead to the role of secular humanists and their control of mass media. Rev. Wildmon has no quarrel with Judaism. Quite the contrary, he has a quarrel with secular humanists and other non-Christians." Reisman adds, "Orthodox Jewry has similar quarrels with Jewish secular humanists and other non-Christians."[47]

Wildmon later acknowledged that his organization has given generous financial support to Reisman's research on pornography.

The question remains: Why does Wildmon note that 59% of Hollywood's elite come from Jewish backgrounds? He not only mentions it, he repeats it ad nauseam.

In his book *The Home Invaders*, Wildmon states, "When the Jewish organization B'nai B'rith honored [Hugh] Hefner as their man of the year, it reflected the shallowness and sickness of those who made the decision, not the religion which gave us the Ten Commandments and, for most of us, our Lord Jesus Christ."[48] Like many anti-Semites, Wildmon has no quarrel with the religion of Judaism, just with the Jewish people.

In a January 1989 *AFA Journal* article, "What Hollywood Believes and Wants," Wildmon stated, "The television elite are highly secular. Ninety-six percent had a religious upbringing, the majority (59 percent) in the Jewish faith."[49] Again, an example of his continuing attacks on secular Jews.

In the same issue, Wildmon published an article titled "Anti-Semitism Called A Serious Problem." The headline leads one to believe that the article is sympathetic toward Jews. In actuality, it creates a diversion and plays upon the prejudices of Wildmon's audience. The gist of the article is that anti-Semitism arises out of the black community!

The article highlights that "Jews continue to be more liberal than other Americans . . ." and specifically points out that "Jews favor homosexual rights more than other Americans." The article stresses that "only 18 percent of the Jews" support a constitutional amendment to allow prayer in public schools.[50]

Wildmon is aware of his conservative audience's homophobia and approval of prayer in public schools. And, typically, Wildmon quotes from the words and findings of others to justify his own conclusions.

Finally, Rev. Wildmon regularly reprints articles by Don Feder, the ultra-conservative syndicated columnist. Although Feder is Jewish, he and Wildmon see eye-to-eye on social issues. Wildmon is quick to point out that Feder "is a Jew." This is another device people employ to mask anti-Semitism, much as racists say, "Some of my best friends are black."

Donald Wildmon's associations

Presented with these insights about Rev. Wildmon, several Christian leaders expressed their concern to the Institute for First Amendment Studies. James Lapp, executive secretary of the Mennonite Church, wrote: "We support Mr. Wildmon in his concern for decency and positive values. We do not support some of his tactics, attitudes or biases against Jewish people."

John L. May, Archbishop of St. Louis, and former president of the National Conference of Catholic Bishops, wrote, "I certainly do not agree with the obvious anti-Semitic bias of Reverend Donald E. Wildmon."

Stuart Lewengrub of the ADL said his group has corresponded with Wildmon about anti-Semitism since 1985. He said the ADL has tried in a constructive way "to lean over backward to give him the benefit of the doubt."

"He's encouraging his followers," Lewengrub said, "to believe that Jews are responsible for the kind of programming they dislike." If Wildmon's point is that Hollywood leaders are secular or atheists, Lewengrub added, he can say so without alluding to their religious background. Nor does Wildmon need to note, as he does, that the Jewish background of television executives "contrasts with society as a whole, which is 2½ percent Jewish."

"There is no doubt in my mind that Wildmon has engaged in anti-Semitism," Lewengrub said. "He didn't stop. He continued doing it."

In response to these accusations, Wildmon wrote, "As far as being anti-Semitic, I am not. I have a Jewish brother-in-law. Also, AFA has supported researcher Dr. Judith Reisman, who is Jewish, generously for over two years. And my Lord was a Jew."

The question remains: Why does [the Rev. Donald] Wildmon note that 59% of Hollywood's elite come from Jewish backgrounds?

Interestingly enough, Wildmon and his ministry are in favor with the *The Spotlight*, a virulently anti-Semitic newspaper. On March 7, 1994, Wildmon's smiling mug appeared in the back-page feature "Spotlight on People." The caption lauded Wildmon's opposition to gay rights, which mirror those of *The Spotlight*.

The Spotlight, published weekly by the Washington, DC-based Liberty Lobby, operates a computer bulletin board service (BBS) called LogoPlex. The anti-Semitism in *The Spotlight* is mild compared to the material appearing on LogoPlex.

LogoPlex is the electronic meeting place of Christian Identity, Aryan Nations, White Supremacists, gun owners, and Christian Patriots. LogoPlex maintains several libraries of articles relating to these themes. Anyone desiring a copy of the infamous and fraudulent anti-Semitic booklet *The Protocols of the Learned Elders of Zion* can download the entire volume to their computer. A popular article available on LogoPlex, "The Synagogue of Satan," claims to expose the Jewish people as being "false" Jews and members of the Synagogue of Satan.

On LogoPlex members can "talk" to one-another via computer, advertise goods for sale, or simply exchange information. LogoPlex also lists over 125 other radical right-wing bulletin boards.

LogoPlex's family forum includes the complete text of Wildmon's latest *AFA Journal*, a list of the AFA's other publications, and the names and addresses of every state AFA director. This enables White Supremacists and other racists to network with the American Family Association.

If people are known by the company they keep, the surfacing of Rev. Wildmon and his American Family Association on LogoPlex says a lot.

Anti-Semitism and Christian identity

Christians who embrace "Christian Identity" believe that there is a difference between "true Israel" and those who call themselves Jews. They think that the true Israelites are today's white Christians, descendants of white Europeans. The blessings promised Israel in the Bible, according to Christian Identity thought, are really for the Christian church. On the other hand, Jews descend from the tribe of Judah, and most who today claim to be Jews are not really Jews, but are Russian descendants of converts to Judaism about 1,000 years ago.

Christian Identity loosely includes Aryan Nations, White Supremacists, the Ku Klux Klan, Christian Patriots, and other related groups. Almost without exception, these groups are heavily involved with gun ownership and "self-defense," and harbor an assortment of bizarre conspiracy theories. This same faction was responsible for the 1984 machine gun murder of Jewish talk show host Alan Berg in Denver.

The rising star of the Christian Identity movement is Pastor Pete Peters of the LaPorte (Colorado) Church of Christ. Peters distributes *The Protocols of the Learned Elders of Zion* and is the author of the booklets *The Real Hate Group* and *Death Penalty for Homosexuals Is Prescribed in the Bible.* Peters—along with Ted Pike (producer of an anti-Semitic video called "The Other Israel"), other Christian Identity ministers, and the Rev. Donald Wildmon—is a popular personality on LogoPlex.

Peters' *The Real Hate Group* depicts Jews as controlling television, the film industry, and the news media. It describes the Anti-Defamation League (ADL) as "the most dangerous hate group in America." Like the *Bottom Feeder* joke book published by Life Dynamics, *The Real Hate Group* characterizes Jews as having large noses.

Peters is significant because he has crossed the line between Christian Identity and more mainstream conservative Christian groups. Besides broadcasting nationally on short-wave radio, he can be seen on the fast-growing Keystone Inspiration Network, of Red Lion, Pennsylvania. This cable TV network is picked up in about 120 cities. Described as a "family" network, it carries Pat Robertson's "700 Club," Jerry Falwell's "Old Time Gospel Hour," Morris Cerullo, James Robison, Benny Hinn, and other popular evangelical Christian programming.

Mainline Christian denominations have a moral duty to speak out against anti-Semitism.

Some have questioned the presence of a rabid anti-Semite on a mainstream Christian cable network. The Rev. Clyde Campbell, Keystone's comptroller, said, "Some people have questioned Peters' presence on Keystone," but said the station previews his programs for anything distasteful.

"Peters is a minister of the Gospel and he does a good job," Campbell said. "Pete says he loves the Jews," Campbell claimed. "The only thing I have against Pete Peters," Campbell said, "is the continual harping on the Old Testament. I think his attitude on killing homosexuals and lesbians is unloving. Jesus provides a better way."

It is important to note that on the few occasions conservative Christian leaders praise Jews, the praise is usually limited to certain ultra-conservative Jews such as Judith Reisman and Don Feder.

In September 1993, the Christian Coalition held a "Road to Victory" conference in Washington, DC. One of the featured speakers was Daniel Lapin, an Orthodox Rabbi. Lapin, reared in South Africa, is a lively and entertaining speaker. As an ultra-conservative, his association with Pat Robertson's Christian Coalition is convenient for both parties.

On a shuttle bus from the conference to the airport, two members of the North Florida Christian Coalition discussed Rabbi Lapin's presentation, and a telling remark was overheard. "He speaks better English than any Jew I ever heard," the speaker said.

At the "Road to Victory" conference, Max Karrer, M.D., who heads the North Florida Christian Coalition, led a workshop called "Using Computers at the Grass Roots." He referred to a particular political race to illustrate Christian Coalition tactics. "As an example of how this works," he said, "we had a legislative race where we had a female Jewish lawyer—liberal, feminist—endorsed by the National Organization for Women (NOW), who had knocked out three years ago a pro-life Christian."

Dr. Karrer's description of a "pro-life Christian" against a "liberal female Jewish lawyer," while brief, smacked of bigotry. This is typical of the kind of anti-Semitism often found in conservative Christian circles.

Anti-Semitism will always exist, but it can do so without popular support. Mainline Christian denominations have a moral duty to speak out against anti-Semitism. When Christian leaders decide to put their foot down, popular support will end.

Notes

1. Gary North, *The Judeo-Christian Tradition* (1989), p.152.

2. *The Sunday Record* (Hackensack, NJ), June 21, 1981.

3. *The New York Times*, February 5, 1981.

4. *The Washington Star*, July 3, 1980.

5. *The New York Times*, April 22, 1981.

6. Jerry Falwell, *Listen America!* (Sword of the Lord Publishing, c.1980), p.113.

7. Christian Broadcasting Network staff prayer meeting, January 1, 1980.

8. *Message of the Christian Jew*, March/April 1994.

9. *Message of the Christian Jew*, January/February 1994.

10. *Eclectic Third Reader* (McGuffey, reprinted by Mott Media, 1982), p.64.

11. *Ibid.*, p.66.

12. *Ibid.*, p.69.

13. *Ibid.*, p.75.

14. *Ibid.*, p.82.

15. *Eclectic Fourth Reader* (McGuffey, reprinted by Mott Media, 1982), p.67.

16. *Ibid.*, p.205.

17. Glen Chambers and Gene Fisher, *United States History for Christian Schools* (Greenville, SC: Bob Jones University Press, 1982), p.38.

18. *Ibid.*, pp.109-110.

19. *Ibid.*, p.112.

20. William S. Pinkston Jr., *Biology for Christian Schools*, Book 1, Teacher's Edition (Greenville, SC: Bob Jones University Press, 1991), p.333.

21. *Newsweek*, May 1, 1989, p.32.

22. North.
23. Tim LaHaye, *The Battle for the Mind* (Fleming H. Revell, 1980), p.142.
24. *Ibid.*, p.143.
25. *Ibid.*, p.147.
26. *Ibid.*
27. *Ibid.*, p.148.
28. *Ibid.*
29. *Ibid.*, p.152.
30. *Ibid.*
31. *Ibid.*, p.158.
32. *Ibid.*, p.159.
33. *Ibid.*
34. *The Truth at Last* #368.
35. LaHaye, p.163.
36. *Ibid.*, p.166.
37. *People* magazine, July 6, 1981.
38. Donald Wildmon, *The Home Invaders* (Victor Books, 1986), p.49.
39. *Ibid.*, p.68.
40. *NFD Journal*, September 1986.
41. *Ibid.*, p.22.
42. November 5, 1987.
43. January 26, 1988.
44. February 22, 1988.
45. May 11, 1988.
46. *AFA Journal*, November/December 1988.
47. *Ibid.*, pp.28-29.
48. *Ibid.*, p.9.
49. *Ibid.*, p.8.
50. *AFA Journal*, January 1989, p.11.

4

Black Anti-Semitism Is a Serious Problem

Joshua Muravchik

Joshua Muravchik is a resident scholar at the American Enterprise Institute, a public policy organization dedicated to preserving private enterprise and limited government.

The relationship between blacks and Jews has deteriorated since the civil rights movement of the 1950s and 1960s. Although black anti-Semitism was present before that time, it has grown in recent decades. The Nation of Islam, led by Louis Farrakhan, is one source of this anti-Semitism. Various factors contribute to black anti-Semitism, including the fact that Jews are more vulnerable than white gentiles to verbal attacks, making them a preferred target for blacks' anger.

As the controversy surrounding the role of Louis Farrakhan in the Million Man March underscored once again, the greatest story of unrequited love in American political life may be the relationship between blacks and Jews.

Jews in the civil-rights movement

When the civil-rights revolution broke out in the late 1950's and early 60's, the front-line troops in the Montgomery bus boycott and then in the lunch-counter sit-ins were all blacks, but among the whites who soon rallied to the cause, a large share—a disproportionate share—were Jews. The Freedom Riders rode in integrated detachments; among the whites, Murray Friedman notes in his recent book, *What Went Wrong?: The Creation and Collapse of the Black-Jewish Alliance*, two-thirds were Jews. A few years later came the "Mississippi Summer," a project dreamed up and organized by a Jew, Allard Lowenstein; according to Friedman's estimate, Jews made up from one-third to one-half of the white volunteers who took part. Of the three martyrs of the Mississippi Summer, two, Michael Schwerner and Andrew Goodman, were Jews; James Chaney, the local activist who shared their fate, was black.

In another new book, *Blacks and Jews*, Paul Berman reports that Jews contributed one-half to three-quarters of the financial support received by civil-rights groups in that era. The organizational support they provided was equally pronounced. The Leadership Conference for Civil Rights, the lobbying coalition that helped muscle all modern civil-rights legislation through Congress, was chaired by Clarence Mitchell of the NAACP, but its director was Arnold Aronson, seconded from the National Jewish Community Relations Advisory Council. This pattern was by no means confined to the upper echelons of the movement; all over the country, Jewish organizations assigned staffers to work on civil rights. In those days, writes Berman, "it was almost as if to be Jewish and liberal were, by definition, to fly a flag for black America."

From Jesse Jackson's "Hymietown" remarks, to . . .
Louis Farrakhan, the anti-Semitic virus has crept
closer and closer to the center of black consciousness.

This was certainly true for my own family. My first visit to the nation's capital took place in 1958, when my parents brought me from New York, at the age of eleven, to the Youth March for Integrated Schools. When the sit-ins began in 1960, my mother and I went to Harlem to join in picketing the Woolworth's on 125th Street. All of the employees and customers were black; most of the picketers were white and, I presume, Jewish like us.

My father devoted his working career to the Jewish Labor Committee; as a matter of course, civil rights were at the top of his professional concerns. My mother's mother, after retiring as a nurse in the early 1960's, trekked each week to the Harlem headquarters of the Congress of Racial Equality (CORE) to stuff envelopes. My younger brother and I both belonged to branches of CORE—rival branches—and across our dinner table we argued passionately about the tactical differences between the two. Mine may not have been a typical Jewish family, but in its devotion to the civil-rights movement, it was not unusual.

Then, just as the struggle for civil rights achieved its cardinal victories with the passage of the Civil Rights Act of 1964 and the Voting Rights Act of 1965, many of its black activists began to turn away from their original goal, taking up instead the cause of "black power." The meaning of black power was never clearly defined. Its driving motive seemed to be the venting of rage over racial humiliation, a rage that the earlier civil-rights movement had insisted on subordinating to the strategy of nonviolence and sublimating in the rhetoric of Christian love.

One convenient arena for this rage was the movement's own organizations, in which the presence of whites in leading positions, and indeed at all levels, was now regarded as an intolerable affront. In a trice, CORE and the Student Nonviolent Coordinating Committee (SNCC), which had been on the cutting edge of the fight for integration, became racially exclusive. For a while, CORE continued to allow my grandmother to stuff envelopes, but in time she was asked not to come back.

With whites in the movement redefined as oppressors, and with so many of the whites being who they were, some of the new hostility was bound to assume an anti-Jewish tone. In 1967, at the Conference for a New Politics organized by leaders of the New Left soon after Israel's victory in the Six-Day War, the black caucus insisted on pushing through a resolution condemning "imperialist Zionist[s]." The following year, during the New York City school strike, leaflets were distributed attacking Jewish teachers as "Middle-East murderers of colored people," and a viciously anti-Semitic poem was read over the radio by the black activist Leslie Campbell.

These developments, cutting so sharply against the fraternal grain of the civil-rights struggle, shocked the Jewish community. Perhaps they should not have done so. For as we are reminded by Murray Friedman, anti-Semitism has in fact had a long history among American blacks. In the 1920's, the "buy-black" campaign of the black-nationalist leader Marcus Garvey was explicitly targeted at Jews, and Garvey later spoke admiringly of Adolf Hitler. Malcolm X, too, was a vociferous anti-Semite in both public and in private. In one meeting with representatives of the Ku Klux Klan, at which he solicited their support for his project of black separatism, Malcolm "assured them," writes Friedman, that "it was Jews who were behind the integration movement."

The growth of black anti-Semitism

"Georgia has the Negro and Harlem has the Jew." Thus did the black writer James Baldwin acknowledge in *Commentary* in February 1948 how widespread anti-Semitism was in his community. In time, Baldwin would demonstrate that he, too, was not above indulging in a little of the practice, as when he wrote that while Christians make up America's true power structure, the Jew "is doing their dirty work." Baldwin went on to denigrate Jewish financial support of civil-rights organizations as mere "conscience money," and to complain bitterly that the Harlem and Watts riots of the mid-1960's were not treated on the same high moral plane as the Warsaw Ghetto uprising of 1943.

Still, Garvey and Malcolm were marginal figures in their time (although Malcolm has loomed larger in death), and Baldwin's tortured formulations, like the outbursts that punctuated the New York City teachers' strike, seem rather tame today in light of the efflorescence of black anti-Semitism in the past decade.

From Jesse Jackson's "Hymietown" remarks, to the rantings of Leonard Jeffries of the City University of New York, to, finally, Louis Farrakhan, the anti-Semitic virus has crept closer and closer to the center of black consciousness. Signposts along the way include the three-day anti-Semitic rampage in 1991 in the Crown Heights section of Brooklyn; the rise in open expressions of anti-Jewish sentiment in black popular culture, as in the lyrics of the "rap artists" Public Enemy and Professor Griff and the characters drawn by the filmmaker Spike Lee; propagation of the malicious and utterly false notion that Jews played a prominent role in the slave trade; and opinion polls showing anti-Semitism on the rise among blacks—especially young and better-educated blacks—even as white anti-Semitism has declined.

Farrakhan, heir to Malcolm X (and also thought by many to be the man behind his murder), has notoriously called Judaism a "gutter religion," and described Hitler as "wickedly great." His lieutenant, Khalid Abdul Muhammed, has gone him one better, suggesting that the Jews deserved what the Nazis did:

> Everybody always talk about Hitler exterminating six million Jews. But don't nobody ever ask what they do to Hitler. . . . They went in there, in Germany, the way they do everywhere they go, and they supplanted, they usurped. . . . They had undermined the very fabric of the society.

Farrakhan's Nation of Islam is a small organization, but even before the Million Man March, it was all too clear that his voice resonated in the black community. In 1984, a full 65 percent of Jesse Jackson's delegates to the Democratic convention said they held a favorable opinion of Farrakhan. In 1988, members of the Congressional Black Caucus gave a standing ovation to Farrakhan when he appeared at their annual convention. When, in 1992, the Nation of Islam published *The Secret Relationship Between Blacks and Jews*—a tract that in the brazenness of its lies and the virulence of its anti-Semitism rivals *The Protocols of the Elders of Zion*, itself now also distributed by Farrakhan's group—the black scholar Henry Louis Gates, Jr. lamented that "it may well be one of the most influential books published in the black community in the last twelve months." And in 1994, when the NAACP under its then-chairman, Benjamin Chavis, insisted on holding a "black-leadership summit" with Farrakhan, it defended the meeting on the grounds of Farrakhan's prestige in the community. After the Million Man March, it is hardly possible to deny that he touches some deep vein in black America.

Explaining the tensions

Not surprisingly, the deterioration of relations between blacks and Jews has caused much anguish—at least among Jews. One expression of that anguish is a burgeoning literature on the topic, with some attempting to patch things up, as in *Jews and Blacks: Let the Healing Begin*, a recently published and quite ludicrous "dialogue" between Michael Lerner, the editor of *Tikkun*, and the black scholar Cornel West of Harvard, a prominent organizer of Farrakhan's Million Man March. Sharing the mystical tongue of Marxism and bonded by a common hatred for America, these two soaring Peter Pans of the 1960's Left look down upon the conflicts between their peoples as so much evidence of false consciousness.

The two books mentioned earlier are more down-to-earth, striving to analyze the problem and its history with some dispassion. Murray Friedman's *What Went Wrong?* is perhaps the most informative and richly detailed history we have of black-Jewish relations in America. It is also a kind of lamentation, one which bends over backward to be fair by rehearsing a lengthy catalogue of both the good done and the sins committed by each group. As for *Blacks and Jews: Alliances and Arguments*, edited by Paul Berman, this is an anthology of writings by black and Jewish authors over the past 30 years. It offers such now-famous essays as Norman Podhoretz's "My Negro Problem—and Ours" as well as more contemporary reflections, including by Gates, Shelby Steele, Cynthia Oz-ick, and others.

With these books in hand, one is tempted to wade into the historical thicket oneself and ask: what, then, accounts for the deepening rift be-tween the two groups—or, to be more precise and more honest about it, what accounts for black anti-Semitism? Why did it reemerge in the very midst of the civil-rights struggle, whose ethos of reconciliation it violated spectacularly? Why has it continued to flourish?

Perhaps the least satisfactory answer to these questions is offered by Berman in his own contribution to *Blacks and Jews*. In an argument rem-iniscent of the tortured efforts by cold-war doves to balance every Soviet misdeed with a parallel misdeed by the United States, Berman writes that the most recent eruption of black-Jewish tensions is part of a general "downhill slide" from liberalism in which both groups have participated more or less equally. While blacks have their Khalid Mohammeds who defend Hitler's policy of exterminating the Jews, an equivalent though "not exactly parallel" phenomenon exists among Jews: namely, neocon-servatism! Black-Jewish amity, in this reading, collapsed under the com-bined weight of black apologists for Nazism and Jewish apologists for Rea-ganism. Here, Berman has abandoned entirely the realm of analysis for the easy temptation of taking cheap shots against old enemies.

A more traditional explanation for the rift, offered by James Baldwin among others, is essentially economic in character: blacks have resented the Jewish shopkeepers and landlords in their midst ("bloodsuckers," in Farrakhan's lovely phrase). But few shopkeepers, and not many landlords, grew rich off the ghetto in the past, and fewer still returned after they were burned out in the urban riots of the 1960's. In the ensuing 30 years, the disappearance of such figures should presumably have led to a diminution in anti-Semitism—assuming the Jewish presence was its root cause. Instead, it has increased.

Still another "explanation" is proffered here by the black historian Clayborne Carson of Stanford, who lays the blame for black anti-Semitism at the feet of Jewish *organizations*—which, he says, are "over-bearing in their insistence that black leaders publicly repudiate isolated expressions of anti-Semitism over which the leaders had no control." This strange inversion—making the Jewish reaction to black anti-Semitism its cause—is repeated by the left-wing black intellectual Derek Bell (formerly of Harvard Law School), who complains that "no other group's leaders are called upon to repudiate and condemn individuals in their groups who do or say outrageous things." But this is truly a damning admission: what other groups' leaders would need such prodding?

Responses to black anti-Semitism

As is common knowledge, those expressions of anti-Semitism that black leaders have been called upon to denounce have come not from "indi-viduals" within the black community but from black leaders and intel-lectual spokesmen themselves. Certainly, if the head of a Jewish organi-zation made outright anti-black statements, other Jewish leaders would hasten to condemn him. They would do this not only because it would be politic, but because they would be outraged. In contrast, one senses that the real reason Carson and Bell and the black leaders they defend have not denounced Farrakhan, and resent being asked to do so, is that they are not genuinely offended by the hatred so apparent in his remarks.

From Bell, for instance, we get insipid euphemisms ("Even those who strongly disagree with some of [Farrakhan's] positions must ask whether the negatives justify total condemnation"), while from Cornel West have come outright rationalizations (Farrakhan, according to West, has spoken positively of Hitler "because he wanted to talk about somebody who created a people out of nothing"). With statements like these, it is hardly surprising that neither West nor Carson nor Bell can offer us any larger understanding of black anti-Semitism and its roots; to varying degrees they are enmeshed in it.

Why did [black anti-Semitism] reemerge in the very midst of the civil-rights struggle, whose ethos of reconciliation it violated spectacularly?

One man to whom we can look for a frank accounting is Henry Louis Gates, Jr., who has had the courage to denounce black anti-Semitism in an unwavering voice. According to Gates, anti-Semitism has become "a weapon in the raging battle of who will speak for black America." Within any politically engaged group, he argues, tactical advantage often accrues to the faction that assumes the role of the greatest militancy and obduracy; Farrakhan has demonstrated the validity of this proposition, and his anti-Semitism is part of that posture. By successfully staking out the most radical political turf, he has thrown more moderate black leaders off-guard. Even those who have not been drawn in must worry that they will be split off from the increasingly radicalized mainstream. (As if to illustrate Gates's point, the NAACP and other groups that had remained aloof from the Million Man March rushed to endorse the "black-leadership summit" announced by Farrakhan and his partner, Ben Chavis, immediately after the event.)

Gates's interpretation of the tactical utility of anti-Semitism is persuasive, but it is only the beginning of an answer. Black anti-Semitism has its source not at the level of political tactics but at a far deeper place in the psyche. Julius Lester, a black writer who has converted to Judaism, has attempted to plumb this region. Blacks, he writes perceptively in this volume, achieve a much greater sense of power when they direct their wrath at Jews rather than at whites generically. For white Americans are in some basic sense invulnerable to anti-white prejudice on the part of blacks. "Honky" may be a linguistic or even a moral analogue to "nigger," but it lacks the same power to insult and to offend, a power that would be vividly on display when the Fuhrman tapes were played before the jury in the O.J. Simpson case. Jews, however, for all their success in America, and unlike Gentile white Americans, feel anything but invulnerable, and harsh words directed at them leave real wounds. Hence the appeal.

One might build upon Lester's argument. No doubt because they have been America's most visible and abused minority, blacks see the world more in racial terms than do whites. With humiliations and insults still an undeniable part of daily life, if much less so than in yesteryear, many blacks may well regard the American ethos of color-blindness as mere hypocrisy. Thus, it is easy to suppose that prejudices based on racial or ethnic distinctions, *including those borrowed from whites*, may live on among blacks with great intensity. The novelist Richard Wright, quoted by Murray Friedman, offers a trenchant illustration of this point: "All of us black people hated Jews . . . because we had been taught . . . that Jews were 'Christ Killers.'"

Among the sources of contemporary black anti-Semitism, envy also surely occupies a significant place. In Berman's *Blacks and Jews*, the black newspaper columnist Joe Wood writes poignantly: "We loved and hated Jews like a second child does the first." This love/hate relation has found its ultimate expression in the far reaches of Afrocentrism, with the claim that blacks are the actual, real Jews, and that they who call themselves Jews are impostors.

Wood's observation may also, perhaps inadvertently, contain an equally telling insight into the behavior of American Jews. Did not many Jewish participants in the civil-rights movement love the blacks as a first child does the second, basking in their role of benefactor and protector, and unwittingly inviting the resentment that is ever directed at the self-conscious doer of good deeds?

Overcoming discrimination

But there is another point to be made in this connection. Envy is a powerful emotion, and certainly, when it comes to the Jews, blacks have much to be envious of. Measured by the standard of material or professional accomplishment, Jews are one of the most successful minorities in America, blacks one of the least. To compound matters, though blacks have suffered far more prejudice and discrimination, Jews too have had to overcome barriers never faced by Gentile whites in America. Yet, on average, Jews are much better off than white Gentiles. The success of the Jews forces a recognition, a painful and bitterly resisted recognition, that prejudice and discrimination are obstacles that can be overcome, and that there is no automatic correspondence between how a group is treated and how it fares.

The success of the Jews forces a recognition, a painful and bitterly resisted recognition, that prejudice and discrimination are obstacles that can be overcome.

In an essay in the Berman volume, Leon Wieseltier observes that in renouncing discrimination, America has "dared both [blacks and Jews] to take yes for an answer." Jews have leaped at the chance. Many blacks have hung back, apparently fearing that to accept the dare is to relinquish an excuse for failure. Instead, they have struck a Faustian bargain with affirmative action. The bargain has yielded them some material gains and some "role models," but at the cost of planting the inescapable suggestion that they are unable to compete on their own.

It is the black devotion to affirmative action in its current form that renders meaningless all the talk of rebuilding a black-Jewish alliance. To be cold about it, Jews and blacks today have very few interests in common. It is true that many Jews have historically taken positions inimical to Jewish interests, narrowly conceived, for example by supporting redistributionist economics, dovish foreign policies, and leniency to criminals. But if Jews have been able to disregard some narrow interests, one would like to think that they cannot disregard a broader, deeper one.

Jews have flourished in America as nowhere else in the Diaspora because it is the most meritocratic society in which they have ever had the good fortune to dwell. The principle of equal treatment has liberated Jews from both the injury and the insult of disabilities that were imposed on them for centuries. In that sense, equal treatment constitutes an "interest" of theirs. It is also, however, a matter of transcendent ethical import. It was under the banner of this idea that Jews flocked to the civil-rights movement, and the same idea constituted the only real basis of the black-Jewish alliance that once existed. For Jews eager to restore that alliance, the asking price today is nothing less than that they renounce the principle of equal treatment.

Still, there does remain one powerful Jewish interest congruent with the interests of blacks, and that is racial harmony. Like everybody else in America, but more so, Jews have a stake in black success, for the deterioration of race relations in general is bound to hold special dangers for Jews in particular. That Jews take their responsibilities in this matter seriously is a matter of long and voluminous record. Which only makes it all the more unconscionable that within the black community, hostility to Jews, whatever its ultimate "explanation," should now enjoy a currency and a legitimacy long since faded from the rest of American society.

5

Anti-Semitism Is Psychologically Damaging

Cherie Brown

Cherie Brown is the founder and executive director of the National Coalition Building Institute, an organization that trains people to lead programs on reducing prejudice and developing coalitions.

The impact of anti-Semitic persecution, especially the Holocaust, has been psychologically damaging for many Jews, including those who were born after the Holocaust. Jewish ritual has been one way of dealing with these traumas, but counseling and support groups are needed in order to help Jews cope with their internalized grief and terror.

Fifty years have passed since the end of the Holocaust. But the scars live on in the daily personal lives of the Jewish people in ways more pervasive and complex than many of us have understood. Among the Jewish people are those of the generation who witnessed—and in some cases were victims of—the Nazi Final Solution. The internalized terror of the Holocaust generation has been passed on to a new generation shaping their personal lives, their politics, and most important, their ability as Jews to see the present as a fresh, new moment filled with possibility. Yet the Holocaust is but the extreme of two millennia of Jewish persecution, a pattern of suffering so enmeshed with our sense of peoplehood that it is incorporated into our religious ritual, the history we teach to our children, and our sense of our relationship to the non-Jewish world. We proclaim, "Never Again," but our worldview, so entwined with the past, ensures that we will never forget. And in never forgetting, we often fail to maintain an objective picture of the present—separate from the traumas of the past.

As a young girl, I sat in synagogue between my parents every Yom Kippur afternoon, glued to my seat as I listened to the readings from the Martyrology service, the recitation of the pious and the saintly Jews who died at the hands of their persecutors. With every graphic reading reminding the congregants of all the suffering that had been inflicted upon

Reprinted, with permission, from Cherie Brown, "Beyond Internalized Anti-Semitism: Healing the Collective Scars of the Past," *Tikkun Magazine: A Bimonthly Jewish Critique of Politics, Culture, and Society*. Information and subscriptions are available from *Tikkun*, 26 Fell St., San Francisco, CA 94102.

Jews, including young children, throughout history, I became increasingly convinced that, as a Jewish child, I was not safe, indeed would never be safe. I choreographed dances to *The Diary of Anne Frank,* I read and reread *The Autobiography of Hannah Senesh,* and silently agonized about whether or not I would have had the courage to parachute into Austria, risking my life to save Jews.

Only in later years did I come to understand the extent to which my secret fears were shared by so many other Jews. In the past twenty years, I have counseled thousands of Jews from around the world on a wide range of issues related to Jewish identity. I found that many of them had trouble sleeping. Others struggled with breathing—sometimes in the form of asthma. Many felt an underlying feeling of panic and insecurity in their daily lives, often without knowing why. Still others had difficulty making life decisions. What has struck me most is that these clients, most of whom were born after 1945, saw their difficulties as their personal problems. Rarely did they associate their individual fears with being Jewish or with the Holocaust. The need for Jews to heal these internalized recordings of terror so that they will not pass them on to the next generation should be a central priority of any movement toward Jewish renewal.

Jewish trauma and rituals

One way that Jews traditionally have dealt with the pain of traumatic historical events is to remember and commemorate them in religious and communal services. The tears shed at the Martyrology on Yom Kippur, the sadness felt at Tisha B'Av [a holiday that memorializes the destruction of the first and second Temples], even the upset we feel about being threatened with extermination by Haman are all incorporated into our community experience in doses that aim to make them manageable, particularly when associated with rituals that reaffirm our fundamental belief in the goodness and ultimate power of a benign Being.

But when the pain of near-extermination is still so fresh in the hearts and minds of so many Jews, these kinds of rituals need to be supplemented with more directed counseling or support groups. In these sessions, Jews would be helped to feel safe enough to grieve openly and face the terror from the Holocaust that has led so many Jews to see themselves still in 1995 as an endangered people, or to experience their everyday world colored by panic, worry, or fear.

To give an example from one counseling session, a Jewish woman was deciding whether or not to have a child. She had agonized for months about the decision. Friends and family offered opinions, but she was unable to decide what to do. In the counseling session, I asked her to give me her very first uncensored thought in response to the question, where are you stuck back in your past? She shocked herself with her response: the Holocaust. Out came a secretly held conviction that although she had, in fact, been born in 1949, she believed that she had been alive during the Holocaust and had been forcibly separated from her parents. While she knew that the fantasy didn't make any logical sense, somewhere deep inside, she was still that small Jewish girl who had listened to stories about the Holocaust (often told by well-meaning adults who themselves were still terrified and had not been given a chance to heal their own grief about what had so recently been done to the Jews).

Young children who hear tragic stories, particularly when the victims of the tragedy are children, do not always make a distinction between what has happened to others and what has happened to them. They quickly believe that they are personally involved in the events—that they were there. And they often feel personally responsible for not being able to prevent the tragedy. Many Jewish children have thus internalized the unhealed terror in the voices and the actions of the adults around them. Even children who were never given specific information about the Holocaust or even about being Jewish, had nevertheless unintentionally had that terror passed on to them, in the generalized message that the world is a dangerous place.

The hostility and brutality leveled at Jews, when left unhealed, can be internalized.

It is not that young children should not be given accurate information about Jewish history, including the Holocaust. But when Jewish history is told in voices filled with terror and panic, it can sound to a child as if the same degree of danger for Jews that existed during the Holocaust still persists in the present. And this is simply not true. Compared to many periods in Jewish history, and particularly when compared with the near-extermination of Jews during the Holocaust, Jews are now living in security. And when we speak to one another as if the world of 1995 is just about as dangerous for Jews as the world of 1933, we are setting up a dynamic that can have extremely negative consequences for our lives, the lives of our children, and for all of our political decisions.

Abuse is cyclical

In numerous counseling sessions with Jews I have found that the passing down of this terror from one generation to the next has led to myriad other destructive reactions. There is a growing body of literature documenting that people who are abused are the very ones who then turn around and abuse others. The all-too-common cry that can be heard from some Jews—how can we, who have been so mistreated turn around and mistreat others—is a misunderstanding of the whole mechanism of abuse. Those who have been oppressed often internalize the behaviors of the oppressor and act them out unintentionally against their own people. Thus, the hostility and brutality leveled at Jews, when left unhealed, can be internalized and then Jews may become hostile, hypercritical, or even brutal to one another. This cycle of repeating the initial mistreatment is one of the most insidious results of oppression. The vicious trashing of Jewish leaders by some Jews, when they perceive their leaders to be adopting policies that, in their minds, might possibly threaten Jewish survival, and the high degree of criticism and mistrust between Jews are manifestations of this dynamic.

To give an example of how this dynamic can operate in someone's personal life, I counseled a young woman who passionately wanted to set up support groups to train other young Jews in leadership skills for work in the mainstream Jewish community. She had already established one support group, but she was having difficulty convening the meetings because she kept getting paralyzed by her anticipated fears of being overwhelmed by criticism from the group's members. When I asked her when in her past she had been surrounded by critical Jews, she sobbed as she recalled memories of her parents screaming at each other with terror in their voices; as a young child, she had been powerless to intervene. Neither parent at the time acknowledged to her—nor did they probably understand themselves—how likely it was that their angry fights were dramatizations of their feelings of terror and helplessness.

The need to separate the past from the present is certainly a central theme in most counseling literature. But what has not been dealt with fully in the literature are the unique dynamics of the Jewish experience. How do we determine which patterns of behavior are in fact rooted in Jewish internalized oppression and the collective traumas of Jewish history and which behaviors are simply individual life problems for those individual Jews? When I began to lead workshops for Jews dealing with issues of internalized oppression, almost every participant initially was convinced that his or her family struggles were unique psychological problems. Through years of leading workshops and listening to thousands of Jews I have come to identify a common set of behaviors—panic, worry, urgency, hypercriticalness, etc—that emerge in so many family stories.

[Jewish] difficulties are not . . . isolated problems but also are a result of a history of anti-Semitism and internalized oppression.

Obviously, everyone has at times been frightened or worried. In fact, at least half of the workshops that I have led have included joint sessions for Jews and non-Jews who wanted to work on being better allies. In contrasting the family stories of the non-Jewish participants with those of the Jews, however, I found a convincing pattern of behaviors and struggles among the Jews.

Each person is unique

As important as it is to identify this common set of Jewish struggles, it is by no means appropriate to assume that all Jews have had the same experience. For example, in my workshops I've had Jews whose parents were anything but overprotective, anxious, or overbearing. Every Jewish person is a unique individual with a complex set of life circumstances. And no one set of descriptive patterns of behavior is accurate for all Jews. Yet the preponderance of so much anxiety, worry, terror, and hypercriticalness in so many Jews cannot be dismissed as the individual problems of a few.

And nowhere is the need to heal the terror more apparent than in Jewish communal political decisions. Why did it require a letter from

Yitzhak Rabin [the former prime minister of Israel, assassinated in November 1995] to every rabbi in North America on Rosh Hashanah 1994 to shake them out of their silence and fears about the peace process? Why did Rabin have to take this extraordinary step and make a personal appeal, asking rabbis to back Israel's struggling peace efforts by giving a High Holiday sermon supporting the accords?

If Jewish leaders living far away from Israel weren't able to step outside of their own internalized fears sufficiently to back a major breakthrough in the Arab-Israeli conflict at a time of heightened hope and new possibility, how much more understandable it becomes that Israelis today, in the face of new acts of terrorism, throw up their hands and want to back away from the peace process. Yet the current situation in Israel calls for a courageous response and a firm commitment to stick with the peace process. It is still the only workable solution, no matter how discouraged people feel.

Living in the present

The present experience of betrayal is nothing like the betrayal of Jews that took place in the Holocaust, even when it feels similar. Israel is not in the same vulnerable position in which Jews once found themselves. The strong feelings of betrayal among Israelis, no matter how understandable in the wake of the recent terrorist attacks, cannot be used as the basis for present political decisions. Terrorism is such a successful strategy for our enemies because it so quickly throws us back into seeing the present as an exact repetition of the traumas and memories of the past, even when the present actually differs significantly from the past. The pull for Jews to see the present political situation through a prism distorted by the unhealed fears of the past can lock Jews into rigid responses that miss the fresh political opportunities and needs of the present.

But it is not an easy decision to live fully in the present. It requires the courage to go back and release all the internalized grief and terror connected with being Jewish. It is time that we convene ongoing support groups for Jews in which they can acknowledge openly to one another the fear and pain from the past. Participants would be helped to release the grief from the stories about the Holocaust they'd listened to (or witnessed directly) growing up; they would be helped to see the connections between the struggles in their current life and the past experiences of Jews. A major contribution of the Jewish renewal movement could be to play a pivotal role in initiating these Jewish support groups in communities everywhere.

Even Jews who never heard stories about the Holocaust would still be an important part of a support group. By listening to the life stories of all of the participants, each person could begin to make sense of his or her own experiences in light of what had happened to other Jews. In the same way that women who participated in consciousness-raising groups in the early years of the women's movement listened to each other's stories and came to understand that what at first appeared to be an individual struggle was in fact a political issue connected to a history of sexism and internalized sexism, so too can Jews, through telling their life stories to one another and releasing the grief and terror from those stories, come to understand that our difficulties are not our isolated problems but also are a result of a history of anti-Semitism and internalized oppression.

We can no longer afford to ignore, personally or collectively, how much, as a people, we are still traumatized by the past. Religious rituals will always be powerful tools to inspire us and link us to our ancient past. But ritual alone cannot heal all the internalized terror. It is time that we admit that our entire people is still in mourning and take the time to heal the collective wounds of the past.

6

Antisemitism World Report

Institute for Jewish Policy Research and the American Jewish Committee

The Institute for Jewish Policy Research is an independent think tank that seeks to influence policy on issues that affect Jews throughout the world, particularly European issues. The American Jewish Committee is an organization that works to ensure the safety and security of Jews.

Most Jews are not seriously threatened by antisemitism, which is still present throughout the world but for the most part is declining and becoming marginalized. Antisemitism remains a problem in some countries, such as Egypt and Argentina, but is declining elsewhere, including Germany and Britain. Antisemitism remains unacceptable in most places, but stronger pressure is needed to keep antisemitism from spreading.

The main features of antisemitism in 1996

This is the sixth year of publication of the *Antisemitism World Report*. The tracking of trends over almost seven years (taking into account when the work began on the first volume and the time of writing of this introduction) provides a unique opportunity to make judgements, based on documentary evidence, about the way antisemitism has developed over a significant period. As in previous years, because of the very country-specific nature of antisemitism, it is necessary to strike a cautionary note when making general statements about the state of antisemitism throughout the world. (An overall positive assessment can appear to ignore serious problems in certain countries; but too much concentration on those problem countries can distort the picture as a whole.) However, the international nature of much antisemitic propaganda, including (especially) material that denies the facts of the Holocaust, and the growing use of the Internet as a vehicle for disseminating this propaganda, means that certain trends in antisemitism are truly global and can therefore be assessed on a global basis.

The evidence in the *Antisemitism World Report* 1997 suggests a further diminution of manifestations and expressions of antisemitism in most of

Reprinted, with permission, from the Institute for Jewish Policy Research and the American Jewish Committee, *Antisemitism World Report* (1997). Available at www.ort.org/jpr/AWRweb/mainfeatures.htm. Please check the website for the latest update.

the categories covered, a continuation of the trend highlighted in the Introduction to 1996's Report. The Internet is a growth area for the "publication" and dissemination of antisemitism, and neo-Nazis and Holocaust-deniers claim that it presents them with an opportunity to achieve a breakthrough in terms of influencing the wider public. In fact, there is (as yet) no evidence to suggest that Internet antisemitism has the power to mobilize antisemites any more successfully than any other method.

In Switzerland, the government and the Swiss banks came under intense international pressure, from Jewish organizations and other groups, to explain what they did with Jewish assets deposited in the country before the Second World War, and with gold and other valuables deposited in banks by the Nazis and which belonged to murdered Jews. There was an antisemitic backlash in response to the allegations, stated and implied, that the Swiss connived with the Nazis or were deliberately less than forthcoming about Jewish assets still held in Swiss banks, but it did not go beyond the general level of antisemitism that currently prevails in Switzerland, and was not as severe as some expected. This may change in the light of the further revelations that have emerged and which have put greater pressure on the Swiss banking and governmental authorities to explain their past behaviour.

The Swiss banks affair highlights one of the principal features of the context in which antisemitism must be assessed today: the absolute readiness of certain Jewish organizations and prominent Jewish individuals to attack expressions of antisemitism or to reveal the antisemitic pasts of public figures, and to mobilize and demand justice for the almost forgotten wrongs perpetrated against them during the Holocaust—the prosecution of Nazi war criminals, the restitution of Jewish property, for example—in the clear understanding that antisemitism may increase as a result. Not only does this indicate a greater assertiveness among the organized Jewish community to stand up for its human rights, it also shows that those concerned dismiss the impact of their actions on the level of antisemitism as of no significance.

Contemporary antisemitism—despite its occasionally violent form and its deeply unpleasant nature—poses little serious threat to Jewish existence.

In most countries covered in 1997's Report, contemporary antisemitism—despite its occasionally violent form and its deeply unpleasant nature—poses little serious threat to Jewish existence. Nevertheless, it still adversely affects the way many Jews relate to the societies in which they live, especially in Eastern Europe where the memory of state-sponsored and controlled antisemitism is still relatively fresh. And even though Jews may not be seriously threatened in most places, the degree of antisemitism present in a country is a measure of its respect for human rights. It is, after all, a mistake to judge antisemitism purely on the basis of its impact on Jews. It is no less to be condemned, deplored and combated in countries where there are few, if any, Jews. Fortunately, overall—with some exceptions and fluctuations—Jews feel increasingly secure in the societies in which they live. They are more ready to speak out uninhibitedly about antisemitism and to manage the consequences, whatever they might be.

The salience of antisemitism for the far right

Given the continued electoral progress of the far-right parties that formally eschew antisemitism, and the lack of progress made by the radical, neo-Nazi or extremist groups that are often openly antisemitic, maintaining the distinction between these two types of groups (although the boundaries are occasionally blurred) continues to be crucial.

The success of the far-right's strategy of working through the ballot box was reflected in electoral results for the Front National (FN) in France and the Vlaams Blok in Belgium, but particularly in Austria, where Jörg Haider, leader of the Freiheitliche Partei Österreichs (FPÖ, Freedom Party of Austria), won the endorsement of the traditionally left-wing working class, as well as that of a far-right electorate not usually motivated to vote in mainstream elections.

The main factors involved in the success of the far right are unemployment, economic uncertainty, crime, anti-immigrant feeling and concern at the possible loss of national identity as a result of globalization and European integration. The most militant, in both far-right and neo-Nazi groups, are unemployed young males, and this applies not only in Europe but in North America, Australia and also the Middle East, where those who are attracted to the Palestinian Hamas and its anti-Jewish rhetoric, which goes hand in hand with violent anti-Israel attitudes, are young men rejected by other social and political institutions.

For both the far right and neo-Nazis the key targets of xenophobia and racism are Roma, Turks in Germany, African Americans in the USA, Asians and blacks in Britain, North Africans in France and dark-skinned people from Russia's Caucasian republics, as well as those categorized as immigrants, asylum-seekers and refugees. For none of the far-right leaders who have been making their way towards mainstream political power—Jean-Marie Le Pen in France, Jörg Haider in Austria, Gianfranco Fini in Italy, Filip Dewinter in Belgium and Vladimir Zhirinovsky in Russia—are Jews paramount. On the contrary, Jews clearly occupy a low place on the list of propaganda targets, and are simply one element of a xenophobic world view. Antisemitism, it seems, has been displaced by other forms of racism and opportunistic politicians recognize its lack of resonance in the current social climate.

This is not to say, however, that antisemitism has no place on the far right. For example, in Austria in 1996, charges were filed on two separate occasions against the FPÖ leader Haider. The first case followed his praise for members of the Waffen-SS at a 1995 meeting of the Kamaradschaft IV. Although proceedings were later dropped owing to insufficient grounds for a prosecution, his remarks suggest that his veil of new-found "respectability" can slip. A second case in Austria involved Karl Schweitzer, the FPÖ national secretary. Following a legal investigation into the desecration of the Jewish cemetery in Eisenstadt (1992), the two men responsible were identified as officials of the FPÖ youth organization who had been recruited personally by Schweitzer.

Nevertheless, we are firmly in a period when antisemitism is clearly a subsidiary form of racism. The actions of governments in relation to immigrants and asylum-seekers in 1996 continued to reinforce the general anti-immigrant climate that works to the advantage of the far right and draws attention to minority groups that are unable to blend so easily as Jews into the mainstream. Developments in the European Union continue to create an even sharper divide between the privileged EU space, in which there is supposed to be free movement for all, and the space outside of the EU, particularly to the East and the South, from which it will become even harder to enter the EU. Far-right political resentment is likely to continue to focus on such groups, and antisemitism will not be an effective mobilizing ideology.

The challenge facing those who monitor and combat antisemitism is to understand the role of antisemitism in this political milieu. Exaggerating its influence is counter-productive; ignoring the far right because antisemitism has become more marginal for it is short-sighted. However complex and contingent a phenomenon antisemitism has become, it remains necessary to keep it constantly under review.

Russian antisemitism: a major element in fringe group ideology

The Russian ultra-nationalist leader, Vladimir Zhirinovsky, is often bracketed with European far-right leaders like Le Pen and Haider. But the Russian political situation is very different from that which prevails in France and Austria. While Zhirinovsky's star has, in any event, apparently waned, it is still in Russia that the largest concentration of fringe antisemitic groups and publications is to be found. At the present time, the influence of these 100 or so extremist groups on Russian society appears minimal. Yet, it is difficult to feel much confidence that the regime of President Yeltsin could successfully come to grips with the neo-fascist tendency in Russian life were it to coalesce into anything like a concerted movement. Meanwhile, evident lack of will on the part of the authorities—political, police and judicial—to take consistently firm action against those who instigate racial and ethnic hostility is a matter of great concern.

The militias

Antisemitism within organized groups is also evident among the militias. Most prominent in the USA, but present also in Australia, the militia movement is fundamentally opposed to government and bureaucracy, which are seen to be encroaching on the rights of the individual citizen. Conspiracy theories, including anti-Jewish stereotypes, are one of the mainsprings of this movement. The *Turner Diaries*, a very popular book in the militia world, also appears among the reading matter of antisemites. The *Turner Diaries* clearly inspired Timothy McVeigh, the former soldier convicted of the bombing of the Alfred P. Murrah federal building in Oklahoma. McVeigh and his alleged co-defendant Terry Nichols both had attended some militia meetings and shared their virulent anti-government ideology. Militia groups claimed that the bombing was the handiwork of the government, creating its own "Reichstag fire".

On the fringe: new strategies and tactics emerging

There is evidence that, in order to avoid stronger legislation against racial hatred, far-right groups, particularly the US militias, are devising strategies like "leaderless resistance", or tactical ideological changes in order to avoid arrest. In Spain, for example, neo-Nazi skinheads in Madrid, according to an internal police report, have adopted a new strategy to cope with police surveillance. They have been gradually abandoning traditional skinhead paraphernalia in favour of that of *bakaladeros*—followers of techno and Bakalao music—whose attire provokes a less negative public response than skinhead gear. The metamorphosis has resulted in a decrease in the number of recorded assaults/attacks perpetrated by skinheads by 30 per cent (as compared to 1995), but assaults by other "tribes" have increased by 95 per cent.

Improved communications have led to increased contact between antisemitic groups in different parts of the world. Globe-trotting purveyors of antisemitism noted in 1996 include French Holocaust-denier Roger Garaudy and Nation of Islam leader Louis Farrakhan, both of whom made tours of the Middle East. British Holocaust-denier David Irving was, however, once again frustrated in his attempt to gain an entry visa to Australia.

Neo-Nazi "industry"

In 1996 the rise of the far-right music scene continued. What was new was the success of several neo-Nazi groups in marketing White Power concerts, CDs, videos and neo-Nazi paraphernalia, particularly through mail order companies. White Power CDs are often pressed by mainstream music companies such as DADC in Austria (owned by Sony), the Taiwanese company Ritek and the American companies Eastern Standard and Nimbus Manufacturing. In Sweden, the success of Nordland and Ragnarock records indicates the way that youth culture is used to promote neo-Nazi ideology. Neo-Nazi symbols cross over into the mainstream. Norway saw the rise of the neo-Nazi mail order company Nord Effekter. It advertises CDs, T-shirts, magazines and other merchandise including antisemitic literature. In France, the most significant mail order distributor of far-right material is Diffusion de la pensée française. It has a mailing list of 40,000 names and a catalogue of 3,000 titles including antisemitic and anti-Masonic material.

Antisemitic manifestations

Continued decline

With one exception, in those countries where antisemitic manifestations are monitored either by national authorities or by Jewish communal defence organizations, a continued drop in the overall number of recorded incidents was registered in 1996. In Germany, the Bundesamt für Verfassungsschutz (BfV, Federal Office for the Protection of the Constitution) recorded 846 antisemitic criminal offences in 1996. This figure represents a reduction of 11 per cent on the 1995 figure. In Austria there were only 8 recorded offences, 4 of which were solved ultimately by the police or in court. Those 8 cases represent a considerable drop from the previous year, in which there were 25 antisemitic offences. In France the Commission nationale consultative des droits de l'homme (CNCDH, National Consultative Commission on Human Rights) reported only slight variations in the level of antisemitic violence compared to 1995; the significant increase in the number of violent incidents from 1994 to 1995 did not continue into 1996. In the USA the Anti-Defamation League's annual audit of antisemitic incidents showed a 7 per cent decline from 1995, the third year running in which the total has fallen.

Australia was the only country in 1996 to register a rise in the number of antisemitic incidents over 1995. The Executive Council of Australian Jewry (ECAJ) received 275 reports of antisemitic violence, intimidation and vandalism between October 1995 and September 1996 (a 12 per cent increase on 1994-5 figure).

The findings on antisemitism are in line with an overall drop in the number of recorded racial offences in Germany, Austria and Australia, but not in France.

We continue to emphasize that, while any overall assessment of the state of antisemitism must take such statistics into account, the shortcomings associated with their compilation render them problematic. The absence of a standard method of monitoring, for example, makes objective comparisons between countries very difficult. In many countries where it might be thought to be particularly important to monitor antisemitic offences, such as Russia, there is no systematic monitoring at all.

Less violence

There is less physical violence in the form of attacks on persons and property and a greater incidence of graffiti and threats. For example, in 1996 in Germany, where the total number of antisemitic incidents counted by the BfV was 846, there were, as in recent years, no recorded murders with an antisemitic motive, and only 10 cases of bodily harm. However, there were 174 cases of antisemitic material being disseminated and graffiti, and 45 cases of damage to Jewish property. In France 65 acts of threatening behaviour or public abuse through propaganda were reported in the first nine months of 1996, as compared to 86 in 1995 and 120 in 1994. Even in Australia, where antisemitism is rising, threats and intimidation rose more quickly than actual violence.

This appears to be a reversal of the situation a few years ago when it seemed that extreme antisemites were increasingly turning to violence. The change must partly be a result of improved policing and intelligence work, which have forestalled potential violent incidents and deterred extremists from undertaking them.

Neo-Nazi gatherings generate offences

The statistics and reported incidents recorded in 1996 suggest that violent neo-Nazi activity, and the arrests that follow, increasingly occur within the framework of fascist and Nazi commemorative events. There are many such anniversaries. For example, the "official" 1996 "Hess march" on 17 August, which commemorates the death of Hitler's deputy, Rudolf Hess, was held in the small central Swedish town of Trollhätten. The anniversary of Hitler's birthday, 20 April, is widely celebrated by neo-Nazi groups worldwide. In France, a series of rallies and commemorative events were held throughout the year, which in effect serve to affirm FN ideology. In April, the FN celebrated the 1,500th anniversary of the baptism of Clovis (a Barbarian chieftain who converted to Catholicism and became the first Catholic king of what was then Gaul), holding commemorative events throughout France. Antisemitic literature was distributed at the rally held in Paris. Another French far-right commemorative date is the annual fête of Joan of Arc held on 1 May. In Belgium the neo-fascist calendar is marked by the annual Iron Pilgrimage in Diksmuide, which in 1996, the 69th anniversary, turned into a battlefield. The Iron Pilgrimage officially commemorates Belgian losses during the First World War, but since the 1970s it has become an international neo-Nazi rallying point. In 1996 6,000 neo-Nazis attended the event.

We are firmly in a period when antisemitism is clearly a subsidiary form of racism.

These occasions often contravene the law in some countries since participants invariably wear Nazi regalia, including swastikas, and distribute illegal literature. They turn easily into occasions of minor violence. The police are of course on hand and either make arrests or video proceedings for later use. (At Diksmuide in 1996, police arrested 131 people for possession of weapons and illegal neo-Nazi literature.)

Swiss banks/Nazi gold

Jewish organizations severely embarrassed the Swiss government with revelations over the country's handling of Jewish assets held in Swiss banks during the war, and gold deposited there by the Nazis that had been expropriated from Jews. The issue is, effectively, whether or not Swiss banks collaborated with Nazi Germany. Some Jewish organizations and journalists expressed fears—as they did also in connection with the trials of Nazi war criminals and the process of restitution of Jewish communal property to Jewish communities in East-Central Europe (see below)—that the Swiss banks affair might provoke a major outbreak of anti-Jewish hostility. Some antisemitism did emerge but less than was feared.

For the far right, the issue has been a confusing conundrum—how to exploit it? So far, they have not found any answer. No doubt the public's lack of trust in banks and the banking system has also been a factor in the lack of exploitation of the issue's antisemitic potential.

Property restitution

In 1996 the issue of property restitution also came to the fore in several European countries. There is no doubt that the response of governments to the restitution issue is bound up with attitudes to Jews. No governments have denied that Jewish claims are legitimate, but some have allowed real or imagined fears of an antisemitic backlash to play a part in the decisions they have taken. Most conspicuous in this regard is Poland, where, since the collapse of Communism, the issue has been on the agenda of successive governments for some years but where progress has been painfully slow largely because those governments feared the reaction of the general population. The year 1996 was when the legislation was debated and finalized, and a law regulating restitution of Jewish communal property was finally adopted by the Sejm, the Polish parliament, in 1997. (There is no law relating to private Jewish property and this remains a bone of contention for some Jews.)

Antisemitism in the Catholic Church is increasingly less apparent.

In Hungary, in October, parliament passed the Jewish Restitution Decree, and the Hungarian government has earmarked over $250 million for restitution. Several committees of inquiry were set up in other countries—for example in Norway and France—and negotiations have been taking place involving the governments concerned, representatives of the Jewish communities and the World Jewish Restitution Organization.

Like the Swiss banks and gold issue, property restitution has the potential to produce significant negative responses; indeed in Poland, and elsewhere, some negative reaction was noted and recorded. Nevertheless, despite the way that these issues can feed antisemitic stereotypes—by linking Jews with international pressure groups and money—there has, so far, been surprisingly little additional antisemitism generated. Of course, restitution is likely to be an issue for some years and pressures on governments may intensify, creating an even greater potential for an antisemitic reaction.

Holocaust denial

Without a doubt, the most significant event of 1996 relating to Holocaust denial concerned the endorsement by one of France's most popular personalities, Abbé Pierre, of a book by the Holocaust-denier Roger Garaudy entitled *Les mythes fondateurs de la politique israélienne* (Founding Myths of Israeli Politics). It caused a national outcry and dominated the media for several days. On 26 April, judicial proceedings were brought against Garaudy for "having contested crimes against humanity", on the basis of the Gayssot Law, which makes it an offence "to bring into question one or more crimes against humanity". Although Abbé Pierre eventually retracted the comments he made about Garaudy's work, the affair reopened the controversy surrounding the Gayssot Law (passed in 1990 as an amendment to the 1881 laws concerning the freedom of the press).

Legal developments

The trend towards introducing legislation to combat racial hatred continues, and in countries where such legislation already exists, its use is growing, even if results are mixed.

Among countries where new laws are now being tested is Spain. A new Spanish penal code became effective on 25 May. Incorporated into the reformed code are articles that: prohibit overt expressions of antisemitism; punish acts that incite hatred or violence, or deny or justify genocidal crimes; add "religion" (alongside race, ethnicity, sexual orientation) as a punishable motive for discriminatory acts. Effectively, police and judiciary in Spain are now able to invoke a legal instrument to interfere with or put a halt to the activities of racist and antisemitic groups. Although the law is yet to be tested in court, the December raid on the Spanish Europa bookshop (in which nearly 13,000 books of neo-Nazi propaganda and Holocaust denial written in English, German and Spanish were seized, along with posters, flags, videos and badges), and the arrest of the bookshop owner, referred to above, was made possible by the new law.

Christian antisemitism

Antisemitism in the Catholic Church is increasingly less apparent. The influence of the current Pope has played no small part in this. Elements within the Catholic church (and in the other churches too) which espouse antisemitism are found mostly at the fringes. Incidents in countries where public expressions of Christian antisemitism are unexpected therefore tend to loom larger. In Egypt, for example, the Coptic Patriarch, Baba Shanuda, made antisemitic remarks in an interview published in December in the mainstream periodical *Musawwar*, entitled "The Prophecy by the Jews of the End of Christianity is a Great Mistake". In it, Shanuda quoted extensively from the tsarist forgery *The Protocols of the Elders of Zion*, claiming that the Talmud was the source of Zionist conspiracies. He concluded that "the *Protocols* say that the Jews must take control of the world by sowing ideas of heresy in it".

In the USA, a principal focus of concern is the Religious Right, whose political success raises fears that an intolerant climate will develop in which respect for the civil rights of Jews and other minorities will be deliberately sidelined in favour of the inculcation of exclusively Christian values.

Militant Islam and the Arab world

The two main sources of antisemitism in the Middle East are militant Islam (embodied in parties such as Hamas) and the state-controlled media of the Arab world. There was certainly no lessening of Islamist antisemitism in 1996, but antisemitism in the Arab media tended to fluctuate. The mix of standard antisemitic images, Holocaust-denial material and antisemitic statements quoted from the Qur'an, as distinct from anti-Zionism and anti-Israelism, tends to reflect the current state of the Middle East peace process at any given time. For example in Turkey, when the first Islamist prime minister in the republic's history came to power, there was a perceptible rise in antisemitic images in the media. However, in recent months this has diminished with an improvement in Turkish-Israeli relations.

Another example is Egypt, where the most common antisemitic image is the hook-nosed, black-robed Jew, sometimes with horns, often conspiring against the Arab world, or the Jew as a Nazi. During the economic summit held in Cairo in November 1996, the government-backed daily *al-Gumhuriyya* published a cartoon of a black-robed Jew entering the conference hall with a briefcase marked "domination plots".

Outside the Middle East, Islamist antisemitism remains a focus of concern in a number of countries, particularly Denmark, South Africa and the United Kingdom.

The fact that the racists and antisemites have embraced the Internet with such zeal has made the task of keeping up with them easier.

With no official state-sponsored antisemitism anywhere in the world, the antisemitism that is closest to government circles and often the most blatant emanates from Arab countries. For example, in Egypt in July 1996, newspapers carried reports concerning an incident that illustrated a modern variation on the antisemitic theme of well-poisoning (showing that traditional forms of antisemitism can continually be given fresh life). According to the reports, students at Mansura University claimed that Israeli chewing gum, smuggled into Egypt from Gaza, had been laced by Israeli agents with aphrodisiacs in order to corrupt young women. Despite the fact that the Egyptian minister of health told a press conference that laboratory tests had found nothing wrong with the chewing gum, a member of parliament alleged that it was part of a "huge scheme to ravage the young population of Egypt".

The Internet

The Internet, which has revolutionized communication across national boundaries, presents a new challenge in respect of the dissemination of antisemitic propaganda. The *Antisemitism World Report* was the first to draw public attention to this problem in 1994 and others have now taken up the detailed work of monitoring racism and antisemitism on the Net and trying to map its extent, forms, style and content.

There is as yet no evidence that this medium is more venal than any other; it simply poses different problems. The quantity of racist and antisemitic material to be found on the Internet must be seen in context. There is such a vast amount of words and pages on the World Wide Web alone that racist material must occupy only a very small fraction of it. Also, it is counteracted by the anti-racist material that is increasingly being made available. Projects such as the Canadian site "Nizkor", which provides material about the Holocaust as a counterweight to Holocaust-denial material, appear on the screen as often, if not more often, than racist sites when word searches are conducted. Keying in "White Power", for example, will produce not only skinhead sites but a huge number of "diversionary" anti-racist sites. There are also technical difficulties in finding far-right, neo-Nazi and Holocaust-denial material, sometimes as a result of sophisticated password systems used by Holocaust-deniers and far-right activists.

What is rarely pointed out, however, is the fact that those monitoring racism and antisemitism have a new intelligence source that was simply not there before. The fact that the racists and antisemites have embraced the Internet with such zeal has made the task of keeping up with them easier. Moreover, it has been of very specific use in official action against extremists. Although extremists sometimes attempt to disguise some of their traffic, they do have a marked tendency to expose themselves—after all, they want to be a mass movement and if they are using the Internet for that purpose, they have to make themselves visible.

Racist use of the Internet may well have other advantages. Although the Internet is seen as free and anarchic and beyond control, nevertheless, the presence of the racists could be seen as an unwitting form of self-imposed social control, both because of the conventions they have to adhere to and the fact that they can be monitored. If "battles" with them are fought out on the Net rather than in the streets, that constitutes an interesting development.

The complexity and vast amount of material to be found on the Internet has made it difficult for governments to introduce legislation that curbs its excesses. One way of dealing with the problem was given publicity in 1996: self-regulation by servers and providers. There were cases of commercial servers prohibiting access to antisemitic web sites or cancelling contracts with neo-Nazis when they were informed of the contents of their pages. This action was taken as a result of a "moral" stance adopted by the servers or after a court injunction had been served.

Country developments

Highlighted below are countries where noteworthy developments—both positive and negative—occurred.

Argentina

Past evidence suggested that antisemitism was in decline, but a clear increase in antisemitism was recorded in 1996. In recent years conditions conducive to the growth and spread of racism, xenophobia and antisemitism were at a low ebb, but in 1996 these had clearly taken a turn for the worse: the combination of peak levels of unemployment, growing inequality of income distribution, the intensified perception of corruption in the government and the discrediting of central institutions, together with the continuing consequences of Argentina's imperfect transition from military to elected rule, provide a compelling background. Although antisemitic attacks have to be seen in the wider context of general criminal activity, for the first time in many years the Argentine Jewish community felt threatened.

Canada

In 1996 the unfolding political situation in Quebec produced disturbing evidence of antisemitic and anti-minority attitudes among some politicians and in the media. Frustration among nationalists over their failure to win the 1995 referendum often resulted in attempts to blame someone for the defeat—Jews were repeatedly depicted as a, if not the, major opponent of Quebec nationalism. By the end of the year Montreal's Jews, in particular, felt that this sudden rise of activity, some of which had antisemitic undertones, had not been dealt with convincingly by the mainstream of Quebec's political, civic, intellectual and religious leadership.

Egypt
Antisemitic books, journals, newspaper articles and cartoons were particularly in evidence in 1996, with the tacit approval of the authorities. There was a marked increase in antisemitic propaganda following the election of Binyamin Netanyahu as Israeli prime minister in May. Also, efforts by mainstream elements and opposition movements to resist the normalization of relations with Israel were often imbued with antisemitic arguments.

Germany
The number of officially-recorded far-right and antisemitic offences continued to fall in 1996—in the latter case by 20 per cent. Antisemitic offences make up approximately 10 per cent of the total number of far-right crimes. While the number of far-right and antisemitic offences in Germany remains by far the highest of any country in the world, this fact must be judged in the context of the country's rigorous monitoring procedures and especially stringent legislation against such offences.

Russia
The threat posed by Vladimir Zhirinovsky, the leader of the ultra-nationalist Liberal Democratic Party of Russia, receded further following the June presidential elections, when he won less than 6 per cent of the vote. A diminution in his anti-Jewish utterances throughout the year was also perceptible. General Aleksandr Lebed, also a defeated candidate in the presidential elections, made anti-Jewish remarks during the campaign, for which he subsequently apologized. There are approximately 100 ultra-nationalist groups, virtually all of them professing an antisemitic ideology, but they remained on the fringe of Russian political life. The level of antisemitic incidents does not appear to have varied from 1995; there was nonetheless much unease among the Russian Jewish community that the police and judicial authorities are not doing enough to apprehend, or prosecute, the perpetrators of antisemitic acts.

Spain
In 1996 action taken against Spain's largest purveyor of antisemitic and Holocaust-denial material, the Europa bookshop in Barcelona, illustrates the variety of methods used to counter racism and antisemitism. The promulgation of the new Spanish penal code in May made possible a raid on the shop, the arrest of its owner and the seizure of thousands of antisemitic and neo-Nazi books, proofs and paraphernalia. But a campaign organized by pressure groups, neighbours of the bookshop and a number of civic associations, the Plataforma Anna Frank (Anne Frank Platform), was also effective when it proposed that the name of the section of the road in which the bookshop was located should be changed to "Anne Frank" so that all the shop's stationery and business cards would carry the name of Anne Frank. A total of 10,000 signatures were collected along with the support of 150 organizations and businesses in favour of changing the street's name.

Turkey
In June 1996, Necmettin Erbakan, leader of the Refah Partisi (RP, Welfare Party), became the first Islamist prime minister in the history of the Turk-

ish republic. Erbakan's appointment raised serious concern since he and his party had, while in opposition, frequently attacked Israel and Jews in vicious terms. Towards the end of the year, however, it became clear that Erbakan intended to maintain the pro-western policies of the previous government. Thus, despite the initial surge of Islamist antisemitism, which had gone hand in hand with the RP's commitment to carrying out Islamic reforms in the political, social and economic spheres, fears that its propaganda would result in an escalation of antisemitic attacks against Jews were somewhat allayed.

UK
For the third year running, a fall in the number of antisemitic incidents was recorded by the Board of Deputies of British Jews, and traditional sources of antisemitic propaganda appear to be on the decline. These developments must be seen in the context of the steady decline in the numbers of unemployed and the steady improvement in the country's economic position. Where there is cause for concern is in the increase in Islamist antisemitic activity, mainly on college and university campuses. This shows that the racism directed by one minority group against another must also be acknowledged.

To varying degrees, certain manifestations of antisemitism intensified in the following countries: Belgium, Australia, France, Greece, Slovakia and Sweden.

Conclusion
Looking back over six years of the *Antisemitism World Report*, it can be reliably stated that there was an upsurge of antisemitism at the end of the 1980s. How different it was to the previous decade we will never know because no systematic global monitoring was taking place of the kind brought together in the *Antisemitism World Report*. But the same historical development—the collapse of Communism—that contributed so greatly to that upsurge by allowing previously suppressed or controlled antisemitism to rise rapidly to the surface in former Communist countries, also led to its decline because it heralded the end of official state-sponsored antisemitism. The other principal long-term development that affected the level of antisemitism was the world recession that began with the oil shock in the early 1970s. This was felt particularly strongly in Europe where a growing sense of insecurity, rising unemployment and the decision of governments to reverse their policies on immigrants and foreign workers led to the development of an anti-immigrant climate-fertile soil for the growth of racism and the far right. Visible minorities were the target of resentment, but antisemitism was also given a boost in Western Europe.

The anti-immigrant climate remains, although it has been mitigated to some degree by heightened social concern about the racism it engenders. The economic situation in Europe remains difficult for many countries—over 18 million unemployed in the European Union alone—but there have been significant improvements. Governments have also, to some degree at least, learned to manage the social upheavals and have, ultimately, not allowed them to destroy social peace. That these forces remain potent, however, is seen in the permanence of the electorally respectable far right.

But what the *Antisemitism World Report* has found during the last two years is that whilst racist activity has remained at high levels and has increased in some countries, antisemitic activity has not automatically moved at the same pace. On the whole, antisemitism has remained static or has diminished. This "de-coupling" is an interesting development. However, as was stated in the Introduction to 1996's Report, "this must not make Jews (or anyone else) complacent or any less vigilant—even if Jews are not under attack there are numerous very good reasons why they should demonstrate the utmost concern for and become involved in activity against other forms of racism". But what is clear from the last six years is that antisemitism does not resonate with significant sections of the public in the way that it once did, that it cannot be used to mobilize anything other than small, extremist, fringe groups, and that one important aspect of the "new" means of packaging and disseminating antisemitism—Holocaust denial, the Internet, antisemitism dressed up as anti-Zionism—is that they have arisen partly because activist antisemites cannot get their message across in the more traditional forms.

Whilst racist activity has remained at high levels and has increased in some countries, antisemitic activity has not automatically moved at the same pace.

What we see, therefore, is a *transformation* in the presentation of antisemitism and in the vehicles used to disseminate it. It is allotted a subordinate position in the politics and ideology of the electorally successful far right, though is patently present in their ranks and among their leaders nonetheless. It is channelled through the new globalized, technically advanced means of communication, in order to sanitize it and attempt to evade legal restrictions. It is disguised as pseudo-academic debate in the form of Holocaust denial. And it emanates most threateningly from non-traditional sources—Islamists in certain Western countries—rather than from elements who claim to be defending "white" civilization and host cultures. Antisemitism is also given breathing space in Eastern Europe through the continued reclamation of a pre-Communist past that entails the rehabilitation of wartime fascist leaders like Josef Tiso in Slovakia and Marshal Ion Antonescu in Romania. This transformation confirms that, in general, the social climate remains inimical to antisemitism but antisemites continue to struggle to overcome it.

The evidence of the last six years also shows the importance of countervailing forces. That antisemitism remains unacceptable can be seen in the vast number of initiatives taken in education and in the law, by the churches and by international institutions, in new organizations set up to combat racism and antisemitism, conferences and seminars, declarations, commissions of inquiry. Furthermore, as highlighted at the beginning of this Introduction, many Jews and national and international Jewish organizations no longer adopt a softly-softly approach to antisemitism; they increasingly beard the lion in its den, no matter what the consequences.

1997's *Antisemitism World Report* highlights points of concern—the antisemitic utterances of Louis Farrakhan, which are not taken sufficiently seriously by significant elements in American society; the propensity for even a moderate state like Egypt to sanction the use of antisemitism in political conflicts with Israel; antisemitism from Islamist sources in western countries; antisemitism on the Internet—some of them quite intractable. But they tend to be specific problems occurring in a climate in which antisemitism remains socially unacceptable. It is conceivable that that climate is changing—there are suggestions that this may be the case in the USA and France, for example—but whether this is a natural adjustment as the Second World War recedes into history, or something more sinister, remains to be seen. Only continued monitoring, analysis and assessment will determine whether this is the case. Certainly, on the evidence of this year's Report the overall trend suggests that the pressures preventing antisemitism from becoming the main global language of racism remain strong, if not as strong as they should be.

7

Israeli Policies Exacerbate Anti-Semitism

Naim Ateek

Naim Ateek is the director of Sabeel Liberation Theology Center, a grassroots movement that seeks to deepen the faith of Palestinian Christians, and the author of Faith and the Intifada: Palestinian Christian Voices *and* Justice, and Only Justice: A Palestinian Theology of Liberation.

Although anti-Semitism is evil, its presence in modern society is partly the fault of Israeli policies toward Palestinians. Israel's unjust treatment of Palestinians, including human rights violations and confiscation of land, has done a disservice to Judaism, God, and humanity.

In the early fifties when John Foster Dulles, then US Secretary of State, was asked about the Palestinians, his reply was, "the parents will die and the children will forget". This was the hope on which many pro-Israel people were banking. The truth today is that most Palestinians have not forgotten. Palestine is still alive in the memory, the psyche, and the hearts of people. As Palestinians watch the peace process collapse and the dream of a liberated state on the West Bank and Gaza turn into a mirage, they are determined to keep Palestine alive in their hearts and minds and in those of their children. Their attitude can be described in this way: let people in power shatter the physical Palestine; let them continue to confiscate the land, drive out the Palestinians, deny them their most basic rights, and shatter every fiber of their dream. Palestinians will continue to live and survive; and Palestine will ultimately emerge out of the ashes. The dry bones will live again. If this was true for Jews after two thousand years, it will certainly be true for Palestinians and in much less time. Israel cannot totally abolish Palestine, it can only postpone its emergence. Palestine will retreat for a time and will be dormant in the hearts of its people and friends until it rises again in the future alive and vibrant.

It is interesting to observe what Israel has done to itself during the last thirty years. In spite of the 1948 injustice against the Palestinians, many

Reprinted from Naim Ateek, "Thirty Years of Occupation, 1967–1997: What Israel Has Done to Itself," *Cornerstone*, Summer 1997. Available at www.sabeel.org/news/newsltr8/index.htm.

people in the world, including the western powers, were able to justify the establishment of the state because of the holocaust. Today, most countries of the world, including most of the western powers, cannot accept Israel's flagrant violations of international law in the occupied territories. The Likud government does not bear all the blame. Much of the political injustice including the abuse of human rights was carried out when the Labor party was in government. The Likud, however, due to its ideology, has for all practical purposes brought the peace process to a halt and acutely heightened the tension. In fact, with the tacit support of the United States, the governments of Israel, both Likud and Labor, have cunningly turned the process to their advantage and made it into another form of Zionism. Therefore, the Zionist dream which they were not able to achieve before the peace process, is being diligently accomplished through the peace process.

During the last thirty years of Israeli occupation of East Jerusalem, the West Bank, and the Gaza Strip, it has been possible for many Israelis to pride themselves on their many successes. One can point to: the strong military power of Israel that has, over the years, reduced the threat of war against it; the giant strides toward a strong economy; the peace treaties with Egypt and Jordan; the end of the Arab boycott; opening of the road for normalizing of relations with a number of Arab countries; the creation of a peace process with the Palestinians that practically and effectively removed the Palestine issue from the hands of the United Nations and placed it in the safe hands of its closest and most faithful ally, namely, the United States; the skillful manipulation of the peace process whereby more Palestinian land has been confiscated, more settlements have been established and expanded; and the success of creating a so-called Palestinian autonomy that is closer to what the apartheid South African government tried to do to the predominantly black indigenous population in the creation of bantustans and what some Palestinians are now calling the "Palestans" for the Palestinians. From the perspective of many Israelis, even the occupation itself has been humane and has helped raise the standard of life for the Palestinians. Israel, it seems to many, has the right to congratulate itself on these and other successes over the last thirty years.

We should not, however, be lured by the magnetism of these apparently impressive accomplishments. In the eyes of people of power, they are undoubtedly impressive. At a deeper level, however, the occupation has left and continues to leave many deep scars of long lasting effect. I would like to mention two major areas where, in my opinion, serious damage has been done that carries alarming ramifications for Israel and Israelis in particular and for the Jewish people in general.

Israel's role in anti-Semitism

Although we condemn anti-semitism and all forms of racism as evil and do not in any way justify it, Israel today has become guilty in creating anti-Jewish and anti-Israel feelings. Due to Israeli Jewish injustice against the Palestinians and the unrelenting state policies that deny the Palestinians their political and human rights, that dehumanize and humiliate them at every turn, many people including Palestinians, Arabs, and expatriates have grown to resent, abhor, and even hate Israel and consequently Jews.

There are many people in the world today who cannot differentiate between an Israeli Jew and Jews in general. The wrong that Israel does gets generalized and mars the image of Jews. With its injustice, Israel is fanning the evil of anti-semitism and exacerbating it. These feelings against Israel are not the product of a deep prejudice and blind hatred of Jews, they are the product of the deliberate unjust policies of the state of Israel against the Palestinians. In other words, Israel has created and continues to create a new type of anti-Jewish feeling for which she alone bears responsibility.

Israel has created and continues to create a new type of anti-Jewish feeling for which she alone bears responsibility.

Israel can no longer credibly lift the ugly face of anti-semitism around the world and expect people to rush to its support and stand with it. It is to blame for what it is creating in the lives, minds, and emotions of the victims of its oppression and discrimination. The longer the occupation of the West Bank and Gaza lasts, the longer Israel refuses to share Jerusalem, and the longer the injustice persists, the deeper the hatred of Israel and Jews will grow and the more difficult it will be to heal and rectify the damage. In the minds of many people today, Israel has created a new justified form of anti-semitism.

A disservice to religion and society

Israel has hijacked Judaism. Some Zionists might believe that Zionism is the best thing that has happened to Jews for thousands of years. For them, it is comparable to the rise of the united kingdom under David. Many people enjoy power and are impressed by it. As Christianity got slowly corrupted when it moved into Christendom, it seems that Judaism has been co-opted by the state and has moved into its "Jewishdom". Judaism today primarily functions in the service of the state. On the one hand, Judaism has been used in the service of the state and has given legitimacy to the oppressive and unjust policies of the state. On the other hand, it has achieved its biblical claims by the power of the state. From this perspective, Israel has corrupted the Jewish faith and Judaism has fallen prey to Zionism.

Israel has done a great disservice to God. It has created an exclusively Jewish "God" that is very repulsive to many Jews and certainly to many other people. It is a set back to monotheism and a regression into tribalism and ethnocentrism. This picture of "God" which has emerged under occupation is that of a racist and a bigot. This is not the finer and more refined picture which some of the prophets had presented. The image of God has been marred.

A settler mother was asked on TV whether it bothers her to live with her children on confiscated Palestinian land. Her reply was simple and straightforward, "If it does not bother God why should it bother me?" God in Israel is no longer the God of mercy and compassion, or of justice and righteousness. It has become difficult for many of us to respect the "God" that modern Israel has created.

Israel has done a disservice to humanity. It has become used to oppressing and occupying another people. It has become callous. It no longer hears the cry of the people it oppresses nor feels the pricking of its own conscience. Over the last thirty years, the Israelis have transformed themselves into oppressors of another people. They perceive themselves as being of a better and more superior race than the Palestinians and believe that the only way that would guarantee their security is to dominate the Palestinians directly or indirectly. The Palestinians have been described by Israeli leaders as "cockroaches in a bottle", "grasshoppers", and "animals". Humanity has suffered as a result of Israeli attitude and practice. Israel has lost its human soul.

Over the last thirty years, the Israelis have transformed themselves into oppressors of another people.

Looking back at the last thirty years, one is struck by the moral retreat of the Israeli state. Disservice has been done to the struggle against anti-semitism, to Judaism, to God, and to humanity. The primary cause is Israel's oppressive occupation of the Palestinian people and their land. The moral toll has been heavy and if the injustice persists it will become heavier. What is needed on the part of the Israeli public is to take a much more active role in demanding the end to the occupation. The challenge before Israeli leaders is to have the courage to pull out totally from the West Bank and Gaza, and accept the basic principle of sharing Jerusalem with the Palestinians. Otherwise, the moral collapse will deepen and worsen. If and when the change occurs, Israel will discover that the Palestinian people and their leadership are ready to enter into a genuine peace that will yield its fruits of security and well-being. In the words of the prophet Isaiah, "Everywhere in the land righteousness and justice will be done. Because everyone will do what is right, there will be peace and security forever" (Isaiah 32:16-17).

Christian America
Is Not Anti-Semitic

Richard John Neuhaus

Richard John Neuhaus is a Roman Catholic priest and the editor-in-chief of First Things, *a conservative religious magazine.*

Many commentators claim that America's conservative Christian leaders are anti-Semitic and are creating a society hostile to Jews. However, America is not an anti-Semitic society. Anti-Semitism has declined because of, not in spite of, the dominance of Christianity in the United States. American Jews should support, rather than fear, the Christian majority because secularism poses a greater threat to the well-being of American society than does Christianity.

With a somewhat wearied sense of necessity one turns, yet again, to the question of what is and what is not anti-Semitism. One does so knowing full well that it will not be the last time. Jewish-Christian tensions and the attendant charges of anti-Semitism are a staple in American public life, and will be that for as long as some Christians view Jews as alien and many Jews view Christianity as threatening. Of course these perceptions feed one another. At a level deeper than the perennial contretemps over anti-Semitism, and in keeping with St. Paul's reflections in Romans 9 through 11, the continuing tension has nothing less than an eschatological horizon. As weary as we sometimes might be of the subject, Christians must continue to pay attention. Jews, given their demographic marginality joined to their societal influence, have no choice but to pay assiduous attention.

The current round of controversies has everything to do with the political shock of November 8, 1994 [when the Republicans won the majority in Congress], and alarums over the perceived ascendancy of the Religious Right. As a result, some Jews have ratcheted up to an almost painful degree their antennae for the detection of anti-Semitism. In early 1995, one of our local newspapers, the *New York Times*, went ballistic when the London *Spectator* ran a little article on the self-described dominance of

Reprinted from Richard John Neuhaus, "Anti-Semitism and Our Common Future," *First Things*, June/July 1995, by permission of the Institute on Religion and Public Life.

Jews in Hollywood. The somewhat naive *Spectator* author thought he was doing nothing more than reporting an interesting circumstance and, as it turns out, was in large part relying on what Jewish writers had said about Jews and Hollywood. The young man did not understand that, according to the rules of the more extreme members of the anti-Semitism patrol, non-Jews are not supposed to notice when Jews publicly celebrate Jewish influence and success. As Ann Douglas has recently described in her acclaimed account of New York in the 1920s, *Terrible Honesty*, the central role of Jews in American popular entertainment goes back to the nineteenth century and, far from being a secret, has been frequently extolled in film and song. With weeks of letters and commentary in the *Spectator*, our British cousins had great fun with this little squall, chalking it up as yet another instance of American hypocrisy about our professed devotion to free speech.

Michael Lind's attacks

Another young man, hardly so innocent, has been doing his partisan best to exploit the political potential of Jewish-Christian suspicions. Some years ago Michael Lind fell in with those notorious neoconservatives and for some time was an editor of the *National Interest* before he decided to unleash his arrested outrage and go over to the opposition. Having secured a berth with Lewis Lapham's *Harper's*, Lind's attacks on his erstwhile friends have been popping up with remarkable regularity in publications large and small. He pushed the button for big-time attention when he rabbled the readers of the *New York Review of Books* with a slashing indictment of Pat Robertson, who, according to Lind, runs the Christian Coalition, the Religious Right, the Republican Party, the pro-family movement, and just about everything else that Mr. Lind doesn't like about America. The charge, as best we can understand it, is that Robertson's vast conspiracy is exceedingly dangerous because Robertson believes there are vast conspiracies.

Mr. Lind thought he hit pay dirt with the 1992 book, *The New World Order*, in which Robertson tells you everything you wanted to know, and more, about how the world got into its present sorry shape. Robertson's eccentric and sometimes bizarre account of modern history gives a prominent role to, among others, "European financiers" who allegedly have been pulling the strings of global politics for a very long time. Lind pounces on the fact that some of the sources cited by Robertson are also cited by anti-Semites who explain modern history by reference to the machinations of "Jewish bankers." That Robertson refers to them as European rather than as Jewish is clear evidence, to Mr. Lind, that Robertson is not only anti-Semitic but is trying to disguise his anti-Semitism. He is the worst kind of anti-Semite, the kind that refuses to criticize Jews. The ever-so-devious Robertson also cultivates Jewish leaders, invites them to speak at his public meetings, and has a Jewish attorney heading his religious freedom organization. Is more evidence of his anti-Semitism needed?

This is not to let Robertson off the hook. True, in justifying his use of notorious sources he invokes the authority of a respectable professor at Georgetown University who uses the same sources, and he notes that President Clinton has on occasion invoked the authority of said professor, who apparently taught him when he was at Georgetown. But none of this gets us anywhere helpful. The fact is that some of the sources employed in *The New World Order* are manifestly anti-Semitic, and Mr. Robertson would have saved himself a lot of sorrow by clearly and explicitly repudiating that anti-Semitism in his book. Even better, he should not have used such sources in the first place. The conclusion remains, however, that while Pat Robertson is guilty of writing bad history, there is no ground whatever for accusing him of anti-Semitism.

Nonetheless, Frank Rich, columnist for the *Times*, picked up on the Lind article to demand that the media dig into the dirt of Robertson's, and the Christian Right's, putative anti-Semitism. Rich has been described as the *Times'* attack dog, which, while not very nice, is apt enough. He comes across as a toy Doberman in perpetual snit. His attack elicited an extended response from Robertson which, to its credit, the *Times* published. Robertson explained that *The New World Order* was written at the height of the Gulf War when he was worried about the compromise of U.S. sovereignty and Israeli safety in a "New World Order" under the aegis of the United Nations. "I do feel," wrote Robertson, "that only someone who is desperately attempting to cause mischief would make the unfounded allegations about me or my book that have recently appeared in the *New York Times*." He continued: "All who know me, Jewish and Christian, recognize that I have been one of the strongest friends of Israel anywhere in the world. In 1974, when Israel appeared threatened and alone as a result of a worldwide oil crisis, I made a vow that I have kept to this day: I promised to use my influence, and that of the institutions I founded, to vigorously support Israel and the Jewish people. I have kept my vow. My comments on my daily television program have been pro-Israel. In fact, during the Gulf War, I was one of the few voices in America speaking out regularly in support of Israel. I have lobbied for Israel, and donated hundreds of thousands of dollars to Jewish interests and organizations. By every public word and deed, I have kept my promise."

> *While Pat Robertson is guilty of writing bad history, there is no ground whatever for accusing him of anti-Semitism.*

Frank Rich was not impressed. A few days later he barked back with a column imaginatively titled "The Jew World Order," in which he notes that Louis Farrakhan accuses "international bankers" of nefarious doings and so does Pat Robertson. So there. "Our two most prominent extremists of the 1990s," wrote Rich, "are both dipping into the same well of pseudo-history that once served Father Coughlin and Henry Ford." This is high hysteria even for a toy Doberman. Pat Robertson has as much in common with Farrakhan as Frank Rich has with ordinary decency. The circle of extremists is extended as Rich notes that, at the Christian Coalition convention in the fall of 1994, "Phil Gramm, Lamar Alexander, and Elizabeth Dole, standing in for her husband, all kissed Mr. Robertson's ring."

Lest he overlook anyone, Rich concludes with the shocking report that Patrick Buchanan wrote in a publication of the Christian Coalition that Robert Rubin, Secretary of the Treasury, supported the Mexican bailout to enrich his old investment firm of Goldman, Sachs. (Rubin, Goldman, Sachs. They all sound Jewish. Therefore Pat Buchanan is an anti-Semite.) Never mind that many critics of the Mexican bailout, including perhaps a majority of members of Congress, claimed that its chief purpose was to save Wall Street from its own investment follies. Never mind that in the very same issue of the *Times* television critic Walter Goodman gave a favorable review to Bill Moyers' role as commentator on NBC nightly news, noting that he injected a note "more populist than partisan" when "he criticized the bailout of Mexico as benefiting mainly [U.S.] investors."

While critics, including some conservatives, believe that Buchanan has in the past toyed with anti-Semitic sentiments, his polemics against the Mexican bailout are solidly within the mainstream of political debate.

Hypersensitivity has increased

As one story triggers another, the *Wall Street Journal* has this big item by Jonathan Kaufman on Jews who see "a rise in bigotry." A Jewish woman in Birmingham, Michigan, reports that parents in her son's sixth-grade class have complained that the children can't sing "Silent Night," and a classmate told her son he didn't like having to learn about Hanukkah. "Mrs. Wagenheim," reports the *Journal*, "watched with growing alarm as Washington politicians proposed reintroducing school prayer." "'I thought I could be like everyone else,' Mrs. Wagenheim says. 'But now we seem to stand out more. I never felt like this before.'" Apparently it has only now occurred to her that 98 percent of Americans are not Jewish, with more than 90 percent claiming to be Christians of one sort or another. If one belongs to a very high profile minority that constitutes no more than 2 percent of the population, standing out should not come as a surprise. It might even be cherished as a distinction.

Rabbi Peter Rubinstein of New York's Central Synagogue says, "To be a Jew is not to be anymore in the mainstream of America. You watch the Republican convention, you read the 'Contract With America,' you listen to talk radio. Before I could have accepted that, as a Jew and as an American, my yearnings were going to be harmonious. Now, I'm not so sure." It would seem that the rabbi's anxieties have nothing to do with being Jewish and everything to do with being politically liberal. For many liberal Jews, however, the two are hardly distinguishable. (Seventy-eight percent of Jews voted Democratic in November 1994.) The *Wall Street Journal* cites other instances of the perceived rise in "bigotry." In Phoenix, Arizona, some Jewish homeowners found advertisements put on their doorknobs promoting a free video on the life of Jesus. A rabbi who represents the American Jewish Committee in Phoenix reports that a woman complained to him that her son was handed a book by a fifth-grade classmate and told, "Read this." The book was about Jesus. Says the rabbi, "People are starting to talk in terms of, 'We are being persecuted.'" A little boy wants to share his faith with his Jewish classmate. Can pogroms be far behind?

The *Journal* suggests there is now a "role reversal" between the Orthodox and what it calls mainstream Jews. Mainstream Jews, it says, never felt anti-Semitism was a part of their lives, while the Orthodox were ever alert to anti-Jewish expressions. This is very dubious history. In the past and at present, it is liberal and secular Jews who chiefly support the hypersensitive institutional alarm systems that flash "Anti-Semitism!" at the suggestion that Jews are not just like everybody else. The Orthodox have always known that being Jewish makes a difference, and should make a difference. There is nothing new in the view of the traditionalist rabbi who, according to the *Journal*, is inclined to "welcoming the religious right and scoffing at suggestions of bigotry." "Moving to the right is a blessing for the country," says Rabbi Joseph Gopin of the Chabad movement. "The government should support religion."

Jews who are astute analysts of the American scene have a similar take on what is happening. William Kristol, the Republican strategist, observes that alarm about anti-Semitism "often does verge into paranoia among Jews." As for his own view, Kristol says, "I prefer the Christian right to the pagan left." Norman Podhoretz, the retiring editor of *Commentary* (Who ever would have thought to describe Norman Podhoretz as retiring?), observes that conservatives don't hate Jews. "They hate liberals. As it happens, most Jews are liberals." Midge Decter's 1995 Erasmus Lecture is titled, "Being Jewish in Anti-Christian America." If the choice is between a dominantly anti-Christian elite culture and the majority culture of Christians, it is suggested, Jews have compelling prudential and religious reasons to side with the Christians.

Another piece of nastiness that has received almost no attention in this country is a controversy generated over Human Life International, a pro-life organization based in Maryland that in the spring of 1995 held its convention in Montreal. B'nai B'rith of Canada launched an all-out campaign against HLI, charging that it is an extremist organization guilty of anti-Semitism. The campaign received major media attention in Canada, and some went so far as to demand that the government stop HLI delegates from crossing the border to attend the convention. B'nai B'rith also pressured the Archdiocese of Montreal, unsuccessfully, to refuse HLI the use of the cathedral for the convention's opening Mass. The prime exhibit in support of the claim that HLI is anti-Semitic is a chapter in a book by Father Paul Marx, *Confessions of a Pro-life Missionary*. Marx is a Benedictine priest and founder of HLI, and in that chapter he deplores the prominent role of Jews in the pro-abortion movement, arguing that Jews, of all people, should recognize the consequences when human life is devalued.

The happy fact, documented by every serious study, is that anti-Semitism in America has dramatically declined in the last fifty years.

The chapter in question may be injudicious, and some points of fact may be disputed, but it is hardly anti-Semitic. No reasonable person will dispute the fact that Jews are disproportionately represented among the promoters of abortion, and drawing analogies between abortion and the Holocaust is hardly "extremist." Without taking a position on abortion, a number of prominent Canadian Jews courageously challenged the slander perpetrated by B'nai B'rith. In this country, Msgr. George Higgins devoted his column, which has a wide readership in the Catholic diocesan press, to the HLI affair. Msgr. Higgins, usually a more fair-minded commentator, accused HLI of engaging in a "flirtation with anti-Semitism," and says that the fact that bishops are associated with HLI makes it difficult for Jews "to distinguish the preachments of HLI from the official teaching of the Church, which clearly condemns forays into anti-Semitism." The Catholic Church does indeed condemn anti-Semitism in all its forms, but, pace Msgr. Higgins, there is no evidence that HLI is guilty of flirting with anti-Semitism. Promptly upon the appearance of Higgins' column, the interreligious affairs office of the New York-based Anti-Defamation League issued a press release commending him for his bold opposition to anti-Semitism.

Anti-Semitism in decline

The happy fact, documented by every serious study, is that anti-Semitism in America has dramatically declined in the last fifty years, and even more so in the last twenty years. It is kept alive at the margins by fringe groups such as Aryan Nation and by racist skinheads broadcasting their hate messages via Internet. Regrettably, it is also kept alive by institutions such as the Anti-Defamation League. The purpose of ADL is to counter defamation of Jews. If there is no defamation of Jews, ADL has no reason to exist. It is an organization that operates by demand-side economics. It has a built-in institutional need for a dependable supply of anti-Semitism in order to maintain itself. Its fund-raising depends upon sustaining a high level of Jewish anxiety about anti-Semitism. One is reminded of a recent report from the Midwest about a volunteer fireman convicted of arson. The village was going to close down the volunteer fire department, and he wanted to provide a convincing reason for not doing so. We do not suggest that groups such as ADL and B'nai B'rith of Canada are deliberately creating anti-Semitism, but by setting off false alarms they seriously reduce the believability of the anxiety upon which their existence depends.

The above-mentioned account in the *Wall Street Journal* reports the views of Daniel Levitas, described as a liberal Atlanta Jewish activist, who invokes memories of czarist Russia. "The Jews used to have a response when the Cossacks came to town," he says. "You close the doors, you batten down the hatches, and you shutter the windows. Eventually the dust will settle and you can come out again. The Jews used to say 'This too shall pass.' This time it's not going to pass." Such sentiments reflect the paranoia to which William Kristol refers and, not so incidentally, are an outrageous insult against non-Jewish Americans. The United States in 1995 is not czarist Russia and the American people are not Cossacks bent upon killing Jews. Whatever his own intentions, statements such as those of Mr. Levitas cannot help but exacerbate Jewish-Christian relations, inflaming anti-Christian feelings among Jews and anti-Jewish feelings among non-Jews.

But he got one thing half-right: "This time it's not going to pass." If the "it" in question is the freer expression of religion and religiously grounded moral convictions in public, a major and lasting change does seem to be underway. Given that this is America, such expression will be predominantly Christian in character. This circumstance is understandably worrying to many Jews, but the challenges that it entails can be explored by Jews and Christians in a manner that does not threaten but strengthens our common participation in the American experiment. This was demonstrated by a symposium at Harvard marking the fiftieth anniversary of *Commentary* at which Midge Decter and this writer, among others, spoke.

In the last quarter century, it was pointed out at the Harvard meeting, there has been a dramatic change among Christians—from Catholics to evangelical Protestants—in the understanding of Christianity's dependence upon Judaism. Not simply the Judaism of what Christians call the Old Testament but the living Judaism that continues in mysterious relation to God's election and unbreakable promise. References to a "Judeo-Christian" moral tradition, for instance, are not merely a euphemistic trope employed to avoid offending Jews, although that may sometimes be the case. There is a much deeper level at which Christians are coming to understand their providential entanglement with Jews and Judaism, an understanding that has slight precedent in the two millennia of interaction between Jews and Christians. This growing understanding should be carefully nurtured by Jews and Christians alike.

From Birmingham, Michigan to Atlanta to the Upper West Side of Manhattan, many Jews have assumed that the more secularized America is, the safer it is for Jews. In this view, Jewish security and success has been achieved *despite* the fact that America is a predominantly Christian society. This view, which is probably shared, at least intuitively, by a majority of Jews, is of relatively recent vintage. An alternative view is that Jews are secure and successful *because* this is a predominantly Christian society. All too obviously, there have been predominantly Christian societies in which Jews have been anything but secure. But the argument is that Christianity in America really is different, that it has internalized the imperatives of tolerance as a matter of religious duty, and that, more recently, it has come to see Judaism as an integral part of God's purposes in history. In a historical study of Jewish attitudes toward "Christian America," sponsored by the Institute on Religion and Public Life, Rabbi David Dalin of Hartford University and Jonathan Sarna of Brandeis University examine earlier Jewish perspectives that are newly relevant to our changing religio-cultural circumstance.

Some Christians are unfairly attacked

It would be a tragedy of historic proportions were the opportunities of this new circumstance to be wasted in politicized rantings against the public assertiveness of conservative Christians. In a time when we are called to be "sensitive" to every grievance and discontent, a measure of sensitivity is due also those Christians who say that they want to take back their country. With the exception of a few kooks on the margins (who bear close watching), people who talk that way do not mean that the country must be taken back from Jews. They do have opponents in mind—"secular humanists," "the pagan left," "the cultural elites," "the mainstream media." In sum, the people and institutions that have in the past portrayed, and still do portray, millions of Americans as dangerous aliens, as strangers in their own land. These newly activated Americans are fed up with being put on the defensive because of what they see as their adherence to Christian belief and morality. This populist resurgence is undoubtedly driven by a degree of resentment, and it, too, may sometimes "verge into paranoia." For the most part, however, it is a perfectly understandable reaction to be being treated with disrespect, even contempt, by the champions of secularism.

As the Jews of tomorrow are more religiously observant, they will also be more socially and politically conservative.

Frank Rich and others of fevered imagination to the contrary, the reaction has nothing to with anti-Semitism. Unless, of course, Jews and Judaism are equated with, inter alia, promoting abortion, eliminating religion from public schools, advocating homosexuality, denigrating marital fidelity, shocking traditional sensibilities, and depicting Christians as potential perpetrators of genocide. Those who slander Jews and Judaism by making such an equation are indeed guilty of anti-Semitism, and it makes little difference whether the slander is peddled by Jews or by Christians.

If our reading is correct, the political culture has been dramatically changed in recent months and years, and more dramatic changes are in the offing. The deepest and probably most long-lasting change is the rediscovery of the free exercise of religion, and the assertion of religiously grounded moral conviction in the public square. This is a change that can be welcomed by both Jews and Christians—as citizens devoted to a free society, and as children of the God of Abraham, Isaac, Jacob, and Jesus. This change is understandably feared by determined secularists, Jewish and other, who are taken by surprise that American history is not turning out the way they had confidently expected. The vibrant resurgence of public religion forces them to reexamine their basic assumptions about America and the course of modernity, which is a difficult and painful undertaking.

The Jewish future

There is reason to believe, however, that the next generation of Jews in America will more readily cope with, and even welcome, the free exercise of religion in public. A new study by Seymour Martin Lipset and Earl Raab, *Jews and the New American Scene*, examines the ways in which Jewish ethnic identity is fast eroding. Given the rate of intermarriage with non-Jews and other factors, it is quite possible that a few decades from now only half as many Americans will identify themselves as Jewish. Jewish identity that is based upon ethnicity, anxiety about anti-Semitism, and concern for Israel is, say Lipset and Raab, a fragile thing. The Jewish future in America will be secured not by "Jewishness" but by Judaism, and Judaism is, most importantly, religion. "The central core of Jewish identity has been religion, even though an ethnic culture is built into that religion. It is that religious core which provides a special edge of separatist cohesion for Jews."

Those who have constructed Jewish identity on the foundation of political liberalism have, according to Lipset and Raab, built upon sand. "Some want to believe that an intrinsic quality of Jewish life consists of such universally benevolent 'Jewish social values' as equality, social justice, and world peace. . . . But however strongly held, most of those social values are no longer particular to the Jews, and have clearly not provided the glue which can keep the Jewish community together." As the Jews of tomorrow are more religiously observant, they will also be more socially and politically conservative. And that is because, as these scholars and many others point out, there is a strong connection between religious commitment and conservatism on a very broad range of questions.

Anti-Semitism is a very serious business. Christians, too, are responsible for seeing to it that it is watched assiduously and countered forcefully. That will not happen, however, if anti-Semitism is equated with opposition to the liberalism that many Jews believe to be the essential core of their "Jewishness." It will not happen if fair criticism of the behavior of some Jews, or many Jews, is recklessly condemned as anti-Semitism. And it will not happen if the dominant voice of Judaism in America is that of secular agencies whose stock in trade is to accuse non-Jews of anti-Semitism. Within American Jewry, there are a growing number of thinkers—including but hardly limited to those mentioned above—who point to a more promising way for the flourishing of Jews and Judaism in America. Jews will decide how their message is received, but the rest of us, as Christians and as citizens, have a deep interest in the revival of a Jewish identity that transcends the political partisanships of this historical moment.

Jews who are indifferent to the religious core of Judaism may, as Lipset and Raab suggest, be assimilated into the sector of secular Americans who are equally indifferent to Christianity. There they may maintain for a time an attenuated sense of ethnic identity, much in the way that others are vaguely Italian, Irish, or German "by extraction." But extraction means separation, and identities by extraction are by definition tenuous and short-lived. The interesting and promising future of Jewish-Christian relations rests with Jews and Christians who, in mutual respect and reverence, seek to discern and obey the will of the One who is, through Israel, the light to the nations, and not least to these United States of America.

9

Don't Blame Christians for Anti-Semitism

Joseph Sobran

Joseph Sobran is a syndicated columnist and the editor of Sobran's, *a newsletter of his essays and opinions.*

Jewish claims of anti-Semitism are attacks on Christianity. These claims stem from the belief held by many Jews that anti-Semitism is never the result of their actions. Instead, many Jews wrongly blame Christianity for the Holocaust and Adolf Hitler's rise to power, and they consequently seek to de-Christianize the world.

In a speech to a Jewish group in America, Israel's Prime Minister Benjamin Netanyahu threatened to "set Washington on fire" if the Clinton Administration didn't stop pressing him to concede land to the Palestinians. The substance of the Netanyahu-Clinton argument doesn't concern me here; what's interesting is the colorful warning.

If any other head of state threatened to set Washington aflame, even metaphorically, it would cause a sensation. When Netanyahu did it, it was barely reported. A friend called it to my attention, deep in the middle of the foreign news on page A16 or thereabouts.

Netanyahu seems to have fallen for the canard about Jewish power—the notorious anti-Semitic myth that the Jews wield disproportionate control over Washington. And nobody seems to be trying to set him straight!

Why not? Could it be that he's right? Of course he's right. Once again we encounter the Great Taboo, which is getting a little silly, inasmuch as everyone knows by now that the Jewish lobby is, if not Washington's 800-pound gorilla, at least in the 500-pound range. Discussing American politics without dealing frankly with Jewish power is like trying to cover basketball without mentioning the Chicago Bulls.

A new book called *Esau's Tears: Modern Anti-Semitism and the Rise of the Jews* by Albert S. Lindemann, published by the Cambridge University Press actually addresses the current Jewish mythology with a fairminded candor that has gotten its author both warm praise and hysterical curses. The *New Republic* gave him a favorable review, while a reviewer for *Com-*

Reprinted from Joseph Sobran, "Two Millennia Later," *Sobran's*, May/June 1998. Available at www.sobran.com.

mentary attacked not only the book, but Cambridge for publishing it.

Lindemann argues in effect that the very concept of anti-Semitism is askew: it assumes that gentile objections to Jews are nothing but prejudice based in fantasy. In fact, says Lindemann, the success of the Jews in the modern world was bound to create friction with non-Jews for all sorts of reasons, with faults, irritations, and misunderstandings on all sides.

Sounds reasonable, in any other context it would sound bland to the verge of tautology. Nobody would write a history of France blaming all France's problems on Francophobia; but that's essentially how the history of the Jews is usually told—"the lachrymose version of Jewish history," as one Jewish historian has called it. We are asked to believe that the Jews have always been unpopular everywhere, but that this is due to no faults of their own. When Israel refused to accept the gangster Meyer Lansky, who claimed the "right of return" extended to all Jews, he moaned: "When you're a Jew, the whole world's against you."

Sometimes this attitude is harmless self-absorption, but it can also lead, logically and passionately, to its own kind of scapegoating. When the Jewish columnist Charles Krauthammer refers to "two millennia of persecution," what do you suppose he has in mind? Clue: A few years ago, in a reproachful column about Pope John Paul II, he referred to "two thousand years of Christian anti-Semitism."

Anyone who follows Ziojournalism soon becomes accustomed to hearing about the woes of the last two thousand years, a period marking the time since the destruction of the Second Temple, but even more closely approximating the coming of Christianity. Why not speak of anti-Semitism among the ancient Greeks and Romans, the Babylonians and Assyrians, even the Egyptians whose oppression of the People of Israel is still commemorated every Passover? Why the persistent suggestion that it's precisely two thousand years old?

We are constantly fed, with varying degrees of subtlety, the idea that Christianity is the source of anti-Semitism.

Because Christianity is the target. We are constantly fed, with varying degrees of subtlety, the idea that Christianity is the source of anti-Semitism and the ultimate cause of the Holocaust. Sometimes this teaching is overt, as in the documentary film featured at the National Holocaust Museum tracing anti-Semitism to the Gospels. More often it's indirect, as in the campaign to blame Pius XII for his "silence" during the Hitler years—a campaign that makes little sense (so many people are silent about so many things!) except as part of the larger effort to link Christianity and Nazism.

The great nineteenth-century Jewish historian Heinrich Graetz once wrote to a friend that "we must above all work to shatter Christianity." Though it's very seldom discussed, the Jewish animus against Christianity goes right back to the beginning and persists to this day. For many Jews conversion to Christianity is the worst of sins. A Jew who becomes a Christian (unlike, say, a Jew who becomes a Communist) forfeits the right to "return" to Israel. I've known Jewish converts to Christianity who were ostra-

cized by their relatives. Jews for Jesus encounters incredibly bitter vituper-
ation and even violence. If not for outside pressure and material dependence on Christian good will, the state of Israel would probably have out-
lawed Christianity by now; it already frowns on Christian proselytizing.

The Gospels and the Acts of the Apostles record the bitter split between the first Christians, all of whom were Jews, and Jewish authorities,
who launched fierce persecution; Jews supported and to some extent inspired Roman persecution of Christians. When Christianity became the
religion of Rome, Christians brought bitter memories of the Jews; in the
Middle Ages, Christians burned the Talmud when they discovered,
thanks to Jewish converts, that it contained obscene vilifications of
Christ. Nevertheless, despite many outbursts of violence, persecution,
and expulsion, the Jews were generally tolerated in Christian Europe over
the centuries and sought to live there. If the whole story could be fairly
described as "persecution," the Jews would surely have had the sense to
avoid Christian lands long before they endured two millennia of it.

The word "anti-Semitism" doesn't occur in the entire Old Testament,
where God himself is quoted as saying things about the Israelites that
would today be called insensitive, if not downright offensive. The word
was actually coined in the nineteenth century by a German, Wilhelm
Marr, who, believing the Jews posed a threat to Germany, founded the
Anti-Semitic League; later he recanted his views. The word came to be pe-
jorative and eventually, in our own time, became a handy label for nearly
anything organized Jewry might dislike.

The mythology holds that "anti-Semitism" has no real connection to
Jews. It attacks them unprovoked. Its cause lies exclusively in the psy-
chology and, especially, the theology of gentiles.

This is the mythology Lindemann is concerned to explode. He by no
means blames Jews for anti-Semitism, but he does insist that its rise is best
explained by the entry of emancipated Jews into Western society, an entry attended by success, ambition, achievement, deception, friction,
envy, fear, displacement, resentment, arrogance, and so forth—in short,
all the normal facets of intense social change and group interaction. The
Jews, moreover, often openly despised the customs, nationality, and religion of the gentiles who had become their nominal countrymen; their tri-
umphs were bound to breed irritation even without bad manners, but
there can scarcely be anything less endearing than the combination of
genuine talent and insolence, both of which the Jews displayed to an extraordinary degree.

Many Jews agreed with the complaints of gentiles and tried, with limited success, to make other Jews see that they were asking for trouble. The
whole story is being replicated today in the Middle East, where the more
extreme Zionists refuse to accept any responsibility for tensions with the
non-Jewish natives of the "Jewish homeland." Such Jews insist that they
are always hated for no reason whatsoever, and see nothing odd or im-
plausible in putting 100 per cent of the blame on the other side.

But if Jews don't provoke anti-Semitism, where does it come from?
Too many Jews prefer to believe it comes from Christianity, from the ancient charge that the Jews bear the guilt of killing Christ. This is the ultimate exculpation: anti-Semitism stems from Christian superstition.

As a practical matter, this means that "anti-Semitism" is basically a code-word for Christianity. Without Christianity, there would have been no anti-Semitism. Note that the term anti-Semitism is rarely applied to the Jews' many non-Christian antagonists from Old Testament times to the modern Palestinians.

On this view, Christianity culminated in Nazism and Pius XII was Hitler's "silent" partner. And so, just as Germany had to be de-Nazified after the war, the rest of Christendom now has to be de-Christianized. Prayer must be driven from public schools and all religion from public life, while the role of the state expands and the state sponsors allegedly secular Jewish causes: Israel, Holocaust memorials, Holocaust "education" in public schools (teaching Christian children that their faith created Hitler), and so forth. And of course abortion, loathsome to Christians, must be both legalized and subsidized.

To the secularized liberal Jewish mindset, the ideal Christian is Bill Clinton. He adroitly simulates Christian piety without meaning a syllable of it, while he pursues the de-Christianizing agenda. Organized Jewry is even more united about that agenda than it is about Israel.

10

Assimilation Is a Greater Problem Than Anti-Semitism for American Jews

Alan M. Dershowitz

Alan M. Dershowitz is a law professor, lawyer, and author. His books include Chutzpah *and* The Vanishing American Jew: In Search of Identity for the Next Century.

Contrary to the beliefs of many Jews, anti-Semitism is no longer a problem in America; the greater danger for American Jews is assimilation. Many Jews are too willing to emphasize their history of persecution as a way to retain their Jewish identity. Since anti-Semitism and its attendant oppression have vanished from most segments of society, this focus is no longer relevant. However, Jewish life is at risk of disappearing because of high intermarriage rates and low birth rates. American Jews need to move toward a more positive Jewish state of mind in order to counter the effects of assimilation.

The good news is that American Jews—as *individuals*—have never been more secure, more accepted, more affluent, and less victimized by discrimination or anti-Semitism. The bad news is that American Jews—as a *people*—have never been in greater danger of disappearing through assimilation, intermarriage, and low birthrates. The even worse news is that our very success as individuals contributes to our vulnerability as a people. The even better news is that we can overcome this new threat to the continuity of American Jewish life and emerge with a more positive Judaism for the twenty-first century—a Judaism that is less dependent on our enemies for its continuity, and that rests more securely on the considerable, but largely untapped, strengths of our own heritage.

American Jewish life is in danger of disappearing, just as most American Jews have achieved everything we ever wanted: acceptance, influence, affluence, equality. As the result of skyrocketing rates of intermarriage and assimilation, as well as "the lowest birth rate of any religious or ethnic community in the United States," the era of enormous Jewish influence on American life may soon be coming to an end.[1] Although Jews make up just over 2 percent of the population of the United States—approximately 5.5 million[2] out of 262 million—many Americans mistakenly believe that we constitute a full 20 percent of the American people, because of our disproportionate visibility, influence, and accomplishments.[3] But our numbers may soon be reduced to the point where our impact on American life will necessarily become marginalized. One Harvard study predicts that if current demographic trends continue, the American Jewish community is likely to number less than 1 million and conceivably as few as 10,000 by the time the United States celebrates its tricentennial in 2076.[4] Other projections suggest that early in the next century, American Jewish life as we know it will be a shadow of its current, vibrant self—consisting primarily of isolated pockets of ultra-Orthodox Hasidim.[5]

Jews have faced dangers in the past, but this time we may be unprepared to confront the newest threat to our survival *as a people,* because its principal cause is our own success *as individuals.* Our long history of victimization has prepared us to defend against those who would destroy us out of hatred; indeed, our history has forged a Jewish identity far too dependent on persecution and victimization by our enemies. But today's most serious threats come not from those who would persecute us, but from those who would, without any malice, kill us with kindness—by assimilating us, marrying us, and merging with us out of respect, admiration, and even love. The continuity of the most influential Jewish community in history is at imminent risk, unless we do something dramatic *now* to confront the quickly changing dangers.

Thoughts on Jewish survival

This viewpoint is a call to action for all who refuse to accept our demographic demise as inevitable. It is a demand for a new Jewish state of mind capable of challenging the conventional wisdom that Judaism is more adaptive to persecution and discrimination than it is to an open, free, and welcoming society—that Jews paradoxically need enemies in order to survive, that anti-Semitism is what has kept Judaism alive. This age-old perspective on Jewish survival is illustrated by two tragic stories involving respected rabbinical leaders.

The first story takes place in 1812, when Napoleon was battling the czar for control of the Pale of Settlement (the western part of czarist Russia), where millions of Jews were forced to live in crowded poverty and under persecution and discrimination as second-class subjects. A victory for Napoleon held the promise of prosperity, first-class citizenship, freedom of movement, and an end to discrimination and persecution. A victory for the czar would keep the Jews impoverished and miserable. The great Hasidic rabbi Shneur Zalman—the founder of the Lubavitch dynasty—stood up in his synagogue on the first day of Rosh Hashanah to offer a prayer to God asking help for the leader whose victory would be good for the Jews. Everyone expected him to pray for Napoleon. But he prayed for the czar to defeat Napoleon. In explaining his counterintuitive choice, he said: "Should Bonaparte win, the wealth of the Jews will be increased and their [civic] position will be raised. At the same time their hearts will be estranged from our Heavenly Father. Should however our Czar Alexander win, the Jewish hearts will draw nearer to our Heavenly Father, though the poverty of Israel may become greater and his position lower."[6]

This remarkable story is all too typical of how so many Jewish leaders throughout our history have reasoned about Jewish survival. Without tsuris—troubles—we will cease to be Jewish. We *need* to be persecuted, impoverished, discriminated against, hated, and victimized in order for us to retain our Jewishness. The "chosen people" must be denied choices if Judaism is to survive. If Jews are given freedom, opportunity, and choice, they will choose to assimilate and disappear.

The story recurs, with even more tragic consequences, on the eve of the Holocaust. Another great Eastern European rabbi, Elchanan Wasserman—the dean of the Rabbinical College in Baranowitz, Poland—was invited to bring his entire student body and faculty to Yeshiva College in New York or to the Beis Medrish Letorah in Chicago, both distinguished Orthodox rabbinical colleges. He declined the invitations because "they are both places of spiritual danger, for they are run in a spirit of free-thinking." The great rabbi reasoned, "What would one gain to escape physical danger in order to then confront spiritual danger?" Rabbi Wasserman, his family, his students, and their teachers remained in Poland, where they were murdered by the Nazis.*

I call the approach taken by these rabbis the Tsuris Theory of Jewish Survival. Under this theory, the Jews need external troubles to stay Jewish. Nor has this fearful, negative perspective on Jewish survival been limited to ultra-Orthodox rabbis. Many Jewish leaders, both religious and secular, have argued that Jews *need* enemies—that without anti-Semitism, Judaism cannot survive. Theodor Herzl, the founder of political Zionism and a secular Jew, believed that "our enemies have made us one. . . . It is only pressure that forces us back to the parent stem."[7] In a prediction that reflects an approach to the survival of Judaism strikingly similar to that of the founder of the Lubavitch Hasidim, Herzl warned that if our "Christian hosts were to leave us in peace . . . for two generations," the Jewish people would "merge entirely into surrounding races."[8] Albert Einstein agreed: "It may be thanks to anti-Semitism that we are able to preserve our existence as a race; that at any rate is my belief."[9] Jean-Paul Sartre, a non-Jew, went even further, arguing that the "sole tie that binds [the Jewish people together] is the hostility and disdain of the societies which surround them." He believed that "it is the anti-Semite who makes the Jew."[10]**

The Jewish pendulum

If the Tsuris Theory of Jewish identity, survival, and unity is true, then Jews are doomed to live precariously on a pendulum perennially swinging in a wide arc between the extremes of persecution and assimilation. As the pendulum swings away from the Scylla of persecution, it inevitably

*As he was being taken to his death with his "head erect," Rabbi Wasserman reportedly said: "The fire which will consume our bodies will be the fire through which the people of Israel will arise to a new life." *Encyclopedia Judaica*, vol. 16 (Jerusalem: Ketet, 1972), p. 362.
** The famed Russian writer Ilya Ehrenberg, an assimilated Jew who considered converting to Catholicism, insisted that he would remain a Jew "as long as there was a single anti-Semite left on earth." Joshua Rubenstein, *Tangled Loyalties* (New York: Basic Books, 1996), p. 13.

moves toward the Charybdis of assimilation. In this reactive view, Jews have little power over their ultimate destiny. Our enemies always call the shots, either by persecuting us, in which case we fight back and remain Jewish, or by leaving us alone, in which case we assimilate. The only other alternative—the one proposed by Herzl—is for all Jews to move to Israel, where they control their own destiny. But most Jews will continue to ignore that option, certainly if our "hosts" continue to leave us in peace in our adopted homelands. In this respect, aliyah (emigration) to Israel has also been largely determined by our external enemies, since most Jews who have moved to the Jewish homeland have done so in reaction to anti-Semitism and persecution in their native countries.[11]

Historically, therefore, there has been some descriptive truth to this pendulum view of persecution alternating with assimilation. Jews have retained their Jewish identity, at least in part, because of tsuris. Our enemies herded us into ghettos, created pales of settlement, discriminated against us, excluded us from certain livelihoods while pressing us into others.[12] We stuck together and remained Jews, resisting as best we could the persecution by our enemies.

Today's most serious threats come not from those who would persecute us, but from those who would, without any malice, kill us with kindness.

But there is more—much more—to Jewish identity than collective self-defense. There is something important that is worth defending. After all, until anti-Semitism changed from religious bigotry to "racial" bigotry—roughly near the end of the nineteenth century—persecuted Jews generally had the option of conversion. Unlike Hitler, our religiously inspired persecutors—the Crusaders, the Inquisitors, Martin Luther, and the pogromists—did distinguish between Jews who converted to Christianity and Jews who did not.[13] Indeed, it was precisely their religious mission to convert the Jews, by whatever methods it took.

Many Jews did convert—some at knifepoint, others to advance themselves. The story about Professor Daniel Chwolson illustrates the latter phenomenon. Chwolson, a Russian intellectual of the nineteenth century, had converted from Judaism to Russian Orthodoxy as a young man, but he continued to fight against anti-Semitism. This led a Jewish friend to ask him why he had converted: "Out of conviction," the great man said. "What conviction?" his Jewish friend inquired. Chwolson responded: "Out of a firm conviction that it would be far better to be a professor in St. Petersburg than a Hebrew school teacher in Shklop." Yet despite the material advantages of conversion, most Jews resisted it. Clearly, those Jews—who sacrificed so much—remained Jewish not only in reaction to their enemies. More than our fabled "stiff-neckedness" was involved. There are substantive principles that Jews have been so stubborn about—that we have been willing to fight and even die for. For Jews who define their Jewishness in theological terms, it is easy to find that principle: It is God's will. For the large number of Jews who are skeptical about being God's "chosen people," the principle is more elusive, but it is palpable to most of us, though difficult to articulate. It is a disturbing reality, however, that for a great many Jews, their Jewish identity has been forged and nurtured by our external enemies who have defined *us* as victims of *their* persecution.

Becoming positively Jewish

Now, after two millennia of persecution and victimization, we may well be moving into a new era of Jewish life during which we will not be persecuted or victimized. If this comes to pass, we will need to refocus our attention on defining the positive qualities of Jewish life that ought to make us want to remain Jews without "help" from our enemies. We must become positively Jewish instead of merely reacting to our enemies.

If Herzl's and Sartre's entirely negative view of the reason for Jewish survival were to persist even as we enter this new era of equality and acceptance, then Judaism would not deserve to endure. If Jewish life cannot thrive in an open environment of opportunity, choice, freethinking, affluence, success, and first-class status—if we really do need tsuris, czars, pogroms, poverty, insularity, closed minds, and anti-Semitism to keep us Jewish—then Jewish life as we know it will not, and should not, survive the first half of the twenty-first century. We have been persecuted long enough. The time has come to welcome the end of our victimization without fear that it will mean the end of our existence as a people. We must no longer pray for the czar's victory out of fear that the end of our collective tsuris and the success of individual Jews will mean the failure of Judaism.

I believe that Jewish life can thrive in the next century, not *despite* the end of institutional anti-Semitism, the end of Jewish persecution, and the end of Jewish victimization, but *because* of these positive developments. The ultimate good news may be that the denouement of negative Judaism—Jewish identification based largely on circling the wagons to fend off our enemies—compels us to refocus on a more positive and enduring Jewish identification, which will be more suitable to our current situation and the one we will likely be facing in the twenty-first century, when Jews will have the unconstrained choice whether to remain Jewish or to assimilate. We may be entering a true Jewish golden age, during which we will prove, once and for all, that Jews do not need enemies to survive. To the contrary: We can thrive best in an open society where we freely choose to be Jews because of the positive virtues of our 3,500-year-old civilization.

I say we *may* be entering this golden age; there are no guarantees. Many Jews believe that the end is near, because increasing rates of assimilation and intermarriage are propelling us toward a demographic Armageddon. A recent apocalyptic article in a Jewish journal concluded that "Kaddish time" is fast approaching for the American Jewish community. (Kaddish is the prayer for the dead.) But reports of the death of Judaism may be premature—*if* we can change the way we think, and act, about Jewish survival. If we refuse to change, if we accept the current demographic trends as intractable, then Jewish life in America may indeed be doomed.

The challenge is to move the Jewish state of mind beyond its past obsession with victimization, pain, and problems and point it in a new, more positive direction, capable of thriving in an open society. For unless we do, we may become the generation that witnesses the beginning of the end of one of the most influential civilizations in the history of our planet—a unique source of so much goodness, compassion, morality, creativity, and intelligence over the past several millennia. The demise of Jewish life as we have come to know it would be a tragedy not only for the Jewish people collectively, but also for most of us individually—and for the world at large.

Internal dangers to Judaism

The thesis of this viewpoint is that the long epoch of Jewish persecution is finally coming to an end and that a new age of internal dangers to the Jewish people is on the horizon. Institutional anti-Semitism is on its last legs as governments, churches, universities, and businesses embrace Jews. No Jew today needs to convert in order to become a professor, a banker, or a corporate CEO. Although anti-Semitism persists in many quarters, today's overt anti-Semites—the skinheads, militias, Holocaust deniers, and Farrakhan followers—have become marginalized. They continue to constitute a nuisance and pose a potential threat, but they do not have a significant day-to-day impact on the lives of most Jews, as anti-Semites in previous generations did. Today's marginalized anti-Semites do not decide which jobs we can hold, which universities we can attend, which neighborhoods we can live in, which clubs we can join, or even whom we can date and marry. We no longer look *up* to anti-Semites as the elites in our society who determine our fate. We look *down* on anti-Semites as the dregs of our society who make lots of noise but little difference.

The time has come to welcome the end of our victimization without fear that it will mean the end of our existence as a people.

As Jews and Israel become more secure against external threats, the internal threats are beginning to grow, as graphically illustrated by the assassination of an Israeli prime minister [Yitzhak Rabin] by a Jew, the growing conflict between fundamentalist Jews and more acculturated Jews, the increasing trends toward intermarriage and assimilation, and the decline of Jewish literacy.

For thousands of years, Jews have been embattled. Surrounded by enemies seeking to convert us, remove us, even exterminate us, we have developed collective defense mechanisms highly adaptive to combating persecution by anti-Semites. But we have not developed effective means of defending the Jewish future against our own actions and inactions. This is our urgent new challenge—to defend the Jewish future against voluntary self-destruction—and we must face it squarely, if we are to prevent the fulfillment of Isaiah's dire prophecy "Your destroyers will come from your own ranks."

We must take control of our own destiny by changing the nature of Jewish life in fundamental ways. The survival of the Jewish people is too important—to us and to the world at large—to be left in the hands of those ultra-Orthodox rabbis who would rather face Armageddon than change the religious status quo. Just as Jews of the past changed the nature of Jewish life in order to adapt to external necessities and to survive the ravages of their external enemies, so, too, must today's Jews change the nature of Jewish life to adapt to new internal necessities and to survive the demographic challenges of intermarriage, assimilation, low birthrates, and the breakdown of neighborhoods and communities.

A hundred years ago, Theodor Herzl identified the "Jewish question" of the twentieth century as the literal survival of Jews in the face of external enemies committed to our physical annihilation—Jew-haters in every nation where Jews lived as a minority. His solution—the creation of a secular Jewish state—was to change the nature of Jewish life in dramatic and unanticipated ways. A hundred years later, the "Jewish question" of the twenty-first century is survival in the face of our internal challenges. Herzl also anticipated that this new "Jewish question" might arise if and when our Christian hosts were to leave us in peace. This is now coming to pass. The solution to *this* Jewish question also requires the creation of yet another Jewish state: a new Jewish state *of mind!*

This viewpoint continues where *Chutzpah* (1991) left off, in exploring the larger issue of being Jewish today. In the concluding paragraphs of that book I issued the following challenge:

> We have learned—painfully and with difficulty—how to fight others. Can we develop Jewish techniques for defending against our own success?
>
> Pogo once said: "We have [met] the enemy and he is us!" As Jews, we have not yet been given the luxury of seeing ourselves as the enemy. There are still too many external enemies who challenge the very physical survival of the Jewish people in Israel and throughout the world. But as we become stronger in the face of our external enemies, we must prepare to confront ourselves.

In confronting ourselves, we must face the reality that the generation of Jews I wrote about in *Chutzpah*—those of us who remember the Holocaust, the creation of Israel and the mortal threats to its survival, the movements to save Soviet, Syrian, and Ethiopian Jewry, the struggle against institutional anti-Semitism—is aging. Our children, who have no actual memory of embattled Judaism fighting for the life, liberty, and equality of endangered Jews, are now the crossroads generation that will determine what Jewish life in America and around the world will be in the coming century. It is to that younger generation of Jews, as well as to their parents, that I address this volume.

Anti-Semitism has declined

The last decade of the twentieth century has witnessed the end of state-sponsored and church-supported anti-Semitism. The fall of the Soviet Union, a nation that, since the time of Stalin, had been a major source of international anti-Semitism, had a domino effect on ending the state sponsorship of this oldest of bigotries. Other nations within the Soviet

sphere of influence stopped espousing anti-Semitism as a matter of government policy. Even most Arab and Islamic countries dropped their
overtly anti-Semitic policies. As a result, the United Nations has changed
its tone, condemning anti-Semitism and reducing somewhat its pro-Arab
and anti-Israel bias. Equally important, the Catholic church—the single
institution most responsible for the persecution of Jews over the past two
millennia—approved diplomatic relations with Israel, thus annulling its
entrenched view that Jewish "homelessness . . . was the Divine judgment
against Jews" for rejecting Jesus. The American Lutheran Church explicitly rejected Martin Luther's anti-Semitic teachings.

---

*The last decade of the twentieth century has
witnessed the end of state-sponsored and church-
supported anti-Semitism.*

Bill Clinton's presidency marked the end of discrimination against
Jews in the upper echelons of government. For the first time in American
history, the fact that an aspirant for high appointive office was a Jew became irrelevant in his or her selection. President Clinton—our first president who grew up in an age when anti-Semitism was unacceptable—se-
lected several Jewish cabinet members, two Jewish Supreme Court
justices, numerous Jewish ambassadors and other high-level executive
and judicial officials. Nor, apparently, was Jewishness a bar to election to
the United States Congress, which has ten Jewish senators and more than
two dozen Jewish representatives, several from states with tiny Jewish
populations.* Though we have still not had a Jew at the top of either party's ticket, it is fair to say that in today's America, a Jew can aspire to any
office, any job, and any social status.

The wealth of individual Jews grew perceptibly during this decade,
with 25 percent of America's richest people being of Jewish background.
(If only earned, as distinguished from inherited, wealth is counted, the
percentage would be even higher.)[14] An American Leadership study in
1971–72 found that Jews represented more than 10 percent of America's
top "movers and shakers in business," a higher percentage than any other
ethnic group.[15] Jews' per capita income is nearly double that of non-Jews.
Twice the percentage of Jews as non-Jews earn more than $50,000 a year.
And twice the percentage of non-Jews as Jews earn less than $20,000.[16]
Jewish charitable giving has increased along with Jewish wealth. Jews are
now among the largest contributors to universities, museums, hospitals,
symphonies, opera, and other charities. "In 1991, the United Jewish Appeal raised more money than any other charity in America, including the
Salvation Army, American Red Cross, Catholic Charities and the American Cancer Society."[17] Yet only one-tenth of Jewish philanthropists limit
their giving to Jewish charities alone, while one-fourth give only to non-
Jewish causes.[18]

A Jew today can live in any neighborhood, even those that were for-

---

* *The Daily Telegraph*, December 31, 1993. *Jewish Week*, Nov. 8, 1996, p. 11, puts the number of Jewish
representatives at thirty-one, while the *Los Angeles Jewish Times* puts the number at twenty-five.

merly "restricted." Jews live alongside white Anglo-Saxon Protestants in the most "exclusive" neighborhoods throughout the country—Grosse Pointe, Greenwich, Fifth Avenue, Beacon Hill. And they have been welcomed into the "best" families, including the Roosevelts, Kennedys, Cuomos, and Rockefellers. Economically, socially, and politically, we have become the new WASPs, as a perusal of the sponsor list of any major charitable or cultural event will show. Indeed, terms such as "J.A.S.P." (Jewish Anglo-Saxon Protestant) and "W.A.S.H." (White Anglo-Saxon Hebrew) have become current in some circles to denote the full social acceptance that Jews increasingly enjoy.[19]

Of America's Nobel Prize winners in science and economics, nearly 40 percent have been Jews.[20] Of America's 200 most influential intellectuals, half are full Jews, and 76 percent have at least one Jewish parent.[21] Jews attend Ivy League colleges at ten times their presence in the general population.[22] It is no wonder that so many non-Jews believe that we constitute so much higher a percentage of the American population than we actually do. Jews today are equal in virtually every way that matters. What could not have been said even at the end of the 1980s can be said today: American Jews are part of the American mainstream; we are truly victims no more.

A misperception

Yet despite these enormous gains, many older Jews do not seem to be able to give up their anachronistic status as victims. A recent book on the American Jewish community notes: "[A]bout a third [of affiliated Jews in San Francisco said] that Jewish candidates could not be elected to Congress from San Francisco. Yet three out of four Congressional representatives . . . *were,* in fact, well identified Jews at the time the poll was conducted. And they had been elected by a population that was about 95 percent non-Jewish."[23]

Nor is this misperception limited to California. According to journalist J.J. Goldberg, "[T]he percentage of Jews who tell pollsters that anti-Semitism is a 'serious problem' in America nearly doubled during the course of the 1980s, from 45 percent in 1983 to almost 85 percent in 1990."[24] Yet by every objective assessment, the problem was less serious in 1990 than it was in 1983, and the trend has clearly been in the direction of improvement.

When I speak to older Jewish audiences, I am often accused, sometimes stridently, of minimizing anti-Semitism and am told that it is worse than ever. Social scientists call this dramatic disparity between the reality of declining anti-Semitism and the widespread belief that it is increasing a "perception gap" between what is actually happening and Jewish "sensibilities."[25] Some of the Jews who believe this are similar in this respect to some feminists and black activists I know, who insist that the plight of women and blacks is worse than it ever was.* These good and decent people, whose identities are so tied up with their victimization, are incapable of accepting the good news that their situation is improving. It is

---

* Among blacks and women, it tends to be members of the younger generation who believe that matters are worse than ever.

not even a matter of perceiving the glass as half full or half empty. They see the glass as broken, even though it is intact and quickly filling up. As the sociologist Marshall Sklare puts it: "American Jews respond more readily to bad news than to good news."[26]

I am reminded of the story of the two Jews reading their newspapers over a cup of coffee in a late-nineteenth-century Viennese café. Kurt is reading the liberal Yiddish-language newspaper and shaking his head from side to side, uttering soft moans of "Oy vey" and "Vey is meir." Shmulie is reading the right-wing, anti-Semitic German-language tabloid and smiling. Kurt, noticing what Shmulie is reading, shouts at his friend, "Why are you reading that garbage?" Shmulie responds, "When I used to take your newspaper, all I would ever read about was Dreyfus being falsely accused, the Jews of Russia being subjected to pogroms, anti-Semitic laws being enacted all over Europe, and the grinding poverty of the Jews in the Holy Land. Now, ever since I take this paper, I read about how the Jews control the banks, the press, the arts; how Jews hold all political power behind the scenes; and how we will soon take over the world. Wouldn't you rather read such good news than such bad news?"

With some of today's older Jews, it is exactly the opposite: they refuse to read the good news, even when it is demonstrably true. They insist on focusing on the "oys" rather than the joys of Judaism, as Rabbi Moshe Waldoks put it.[27] This is understandable, in light of the long history of persecution. Like an individual victim of a violent crime who sees his assailant around every corner, the Jewish people have been traumatized by our unrelenting victimization at the hands of Jew-haters. It is impossible for anyone who did not personally experience the Holocaust, or the other repeated assaults on Jewish life throughout our history, to comprehend what it must have been like to be victimized by unrelenting persecution based on primitive Jew-hating. We continue to see anti-Semitism even where it has ceased to exist, or we exaggerate it where it continues to exist in marginalized form. Indeed, some Jewish newspapers refuse to print, and some Jewish organizations refuse to acknowledge, the good news, lest they risk alienating their readerships or losing their membership. For example, in November of 1996 I saw a fundraising letter from a Jewish organization which claimed that "anti-Semitism . . . appears to be growing more robust, more strident, more vicious—*and* more 'respectable.'" Well-intentioned as this organization is, it seeks support by exaggerating the threats we currently face and by comparing them to those we faced during the Holocaust.

The causes of contemporary assimilation

My students, my children, my friends' children—our next generation— understand our new status: they do not want to be regarded as victims. They do not feel persecuted, discriminated against, or powerless. They want to read the new good news, not the old bad news. A 1988 poll of Jewish students at Dartmouth College made the point compellingly: When asked whether they believed that their Jewishness would in any way hamper their future success, not a single student answered in the affirmative. That is the current reality, and it is different from the reality my parents faced—and even from the reality many of my generation perceived when we were in college or beginning our careers. The coming generation of Jewish adults will not remain Jews *because* of our enemies or because of our perceived status as victims.* They crave a more positive, affirmative, contemporary, and relevant Jewish identity. Unless we move beyond victimization and toward a new Jewish state of mind, many of them will abandon Judaism as not relevant to their current concerns.

Jews do not convert to Christianity; they "convert" to mainstream Americanism.

If we are to counteract this trend, we must understand the dynamics of contemporary assimilation and not confuse them with past episodes of assimilation, which were based largely on the perceived need to escape from the "burdens" of Jewish identification. Today, there are no burdens from which to escape. Being Jewish is easy, at least in relation to external burdens. Jews today assimilate not because Christianity or Islam is "better" or "easier," but because Jewish life does not have a strong enough positive appeal to offset the inertial drift toward the common denominator. Jews do not convert to Christianity; they "convert" to mainstream Americanism, which is the American "religion" closest to Judaism. They see no reason not to follow their heart in marriage, their convenience in neighborhoods, their economic opportunities in jobs, their educational advantages in schools, their conscience in philosophy, and their preferences in lifestyle. Most Jews who assimilate do not feel that they are giving up anything by abandoning a Jewishness they know little about. They associate the Judaism they are abandoning with inconvenient rituals and rules that have no meaning to them. As one young woman remembers her Jewishness: "An old man saying no."[28]

We must recognize that many of the factors which have fueled current assimilation and intermarriage are *positive* developments for *individual* Jews: acceptance, wealth, opportunity. Most Jews do not want to impede these developments. Indeed, they want to encourage them. For that reason, we must accept the reality that many Jews will continue to marry non-Jews, but we should not regard it as inevitable that these marriages will necessarily lead to total assimilation. We can take positive steps to stem that tide—but it will take a change in attitude toward mixed marriages, and indeed toward the tribalism that has understandably characterized Jewish attitudes toward outsiders for so much of our history.

Notes

1. Yehuda Rosenman, "Research on the Jewish Family and Jewish Education," in *Facing the Future: Essays on Contemporary Jewish Life,* ed. Steven Bayme (New York: Ktav, 1989), p. 156. According to Seymour Martin Lipset, in *American Exceptionalism: A Double-Edged Sword* (New York: W. W. Norton, 1996), the average American Jewish woman bears 1.1 children (p. 175).

---

*In response to this generational perception gap, one of my students suggested that I title this book *Ghetto-ver It!*

2. There is significant dispute over this figure because it depends on the definition of who is counted as a Jew. If one included only Jews as defined by Orthodox and Conservative religious laws, the number would be lower. J. J. Goldberg, in *Jewish Power* (Reading, Mass.: Addison-Wesley, 1996), puts the percentage at 2.5. He also cites one expert who says that there are 8 million members of the "Jewish political community," in which he includes non-Jewish spouses and children of Jews (p. 57).

3. A 1992 survey by Martilla & Kiley for the Anti-Defamation League found the median estimate by gentiles of the size of the U.S. Jewish population to be slightly lower, but still whopping, at 18 percent. The study also found that only 10 percent of gentile Americans believe that Jews constitute less than 5 percent of the U.S. population. See Lipset, p. 151; see also Goldberg. Mark Twain noticed the disparity between the tiny number of actual Jews and their enormous perceived influence in a remarkable essay in *Harper's Monthly*, September 1899.

4. Elihu Bergman, "The American Jewish Population Erosion," *Midstream*, October 1977, pp. 9–19.

5. As a deliberate survival strategy, America's ultra-Orthodox Jews attempt "to recreate the world that had existed in pre-war Europe" (Jerome R. Mintz, *Hasidic People: A Place in the New World* [Cambridge, Mass.: Harvard University Press, 1992], p. 29). To this end, they take pains to keep secular American influences at bay. Rabbi Elliot Kohn of Kiryas Joel, a Hasidic village in the foothills of upstate New York, explains, "We want isolation. That's why we have no TV's or radios," and that is why such communities use the Yiddish tongue rather than English, dress distinctively, and eschew secular studies (quoted in Don Lattin, "Church-State Conflict in a Jewish Town," *San Francisco Chronicle*, March 25, 1994, p. A1). See also Marc D. Stern, "Orthodoxy in America: The Trend Toward Separatism," *Congress Monthly* (New York: American Jewish Congress), January 1992, pp. 10–12; Egon Mayer, *From Suburb to Shtetl: The Jews of Boro Park* (Philadelphia: Temple University Press, 1979).

6. Simon Dubnow, *History of the Jews in Russia and Poland*, trans. I. Friedlander (1916; reprint, New York: Ktav, 1975), pp. 356–57.

7. Theodor Herzl, *The Jewish State*, trans. Jacob M. Alkow (1896; reprint, New York: Dover, 1988), p. 92.

8. Ibid., p. 91.

9. Albert Einstein, *About Zionism: Speeches and Letters*, trans. Leo Simon (New York: Macmillan, 1931), p. 33.

10. Jean-Paul Sartre, *Anti-Semite and Jew: An Exploration of the Etiology of Hate*, trans. George J. Becker (1948; reprint, New York: Schocken Books, 1995), pp. 69, 91. It should be noted that Christian theological anti-Semites had long espoused a version of this argument. The Apostle Paul was the first to enunciate a doctrine that Jews survive not because of the strength of their faith, their culture, or their ethnic cohesiveness, but rather because God preserves them in a wretched state, by reason of what one might term divine anti-Semitism. Saint Augustine elaborated that God maintains the Jews as wretches and *as* Jews in order to bear out scriptural prophecies about punishing the Jews for rejecting Jesus (see Augustine, *The City of God*, trans. Marcus Dods [New York: Random House, 1950], pp. 656–58). Similarly, the very devout Pascal wrote in *Pensées* that Jesus

preserves Jews in such impossibly abject conditions in order to prove his omnipotence generation after generation.

11. Today, 4.6 million Jews live in Israel, a number that is growing thanks to immigration by former Soviet Jews and the positive Jewish birthrate in Israel, which contrasts with the negative birthrate of every Diaspora Jewish community in the world. Israel is thus well on its way to surpassing America in its Jewish population. (To get a sense of Israel's dynamic growth rate, consider that only 600,000 Jews lived there in 1948.) Demographers predict that in the near future, the majority of the world's Jews will reside in Israel, for the first time since the destruction of the Second Temple nearly two thousand years ago (see Herb Keinon, "In 10 Years, Most Jews Will Be Living in Israel," *Jerusalem Post,* Jan. 7, 1991).

12. Dubnow, passim.

13. Spain distinguished in practice, though perhaps not in theory. The forced conversions attendant upon the Christian "reconquest" of Iberia involved massive Jewish populations, and many converts practiced Judaism in secret—the Spanish called them Marranos, meaning "swine." As a result, Spanish clergy came to view *all* Jewish converts with suspicion. In 1449, the *estatuto de limpieza de sangre* ("the statute of purity of blood") was enacted, which barred converts and their progeny from holding positions in the church hierarchy. This was Europe's first "racial" anti-Semitic legislation: even Christians in good faith, generations removed from ancestors who converted from Judaism, were denied certain rights on the basis of their "blood." A Spanish pope, Alexander VI, decreed the *limpieza* law to be in force in all Christendom in 1495. His successor, the Italian pope Julius II, quickly abolished the "purity of blood" sanctions against Christians of Jewish descent, decrying distinctions based on race rather than religion as "detestable customs and real corruption." Nevertheless, the "purity of blood" policy became even more widespread in Spain, "until it dominated all Spanish ecclesiastical organizations—and, through them, also a major part of Spain's public opinion" (Benzion Netanyahu, *The Origins of the Inquisition in Fifteenth Century Spain* [New York: Random House, 1995], p. 1063. See also Bernard Lewis, *Semites and Anti-Semites: An Inquiry into Conflict and Prejudice* [New York: W.W. Norton, 1986], pp. 82–84).

14. *Forbes,* Oct. 14, 1996, pp. 100–295. A perusal of the 1996 *Forbes* list of the four hundred richest people in America makes it clear how difficult it will soon be to identify people by their Jewish background. But by any standard, the number of Jews on the list is highly disproportionate to their percentage in the population. Even if one were to count only Jews who strongly identify with their heritage—such as Wexner, Soros, Spielberg, Milken, Fisher, Taubman, Pritzker, Bronfman, Lauder, Perlman, Tisch, Le Frak, Lee, Geffen, Lauren, Stern, Rich, Green, Heyman, Peltz, Wasserman, Redstone, and others too numerous to list here—the percentage is amazing.

15. Seymour Martin Lipset and Earl Raab, *Jews and the New American Scene* (Cambridge, Mass.: Harvard University Press, 1995), p. 26. The study was conducted in 1971–72. The percentage is higher now.

16. Steven Cohen, *The Dimensions of American Jewish Liberalism* (New York: American Jewish Congress, 1989), pp. 28–29.

17. Barry A. Kosmin, *The Dimensions of Contemporary Jewish Philanthropy*

(New York: Council of Jewish Federations), p. 28. See also *Los Angeles Times*, Nov. 2, 1992. The UJA replaced the Salvation Army at the top of the Philanthropy 400, an annual ranking of nonprofit groups by the *Chronicle of Philanthropy*. The UJA raised $668.1 million in 1991, up 57 percent from the preceding year. Most of the money helped resettle Soviet Jews.

18. This finding by the National Jewish Population Survey of 1990 reflects the widespread Jewish distaste for nonuniversalist Jewish charities. A 1989 survey of American Jewish attitudes toward Jewish identity revealed that 31 percent of American Jews believe that "Jewish charities and organizations place too much emphasis on helping only Jews and not enough on helping all people in need whether they're Jewish or not" (Steven M. Cohen, *Content or Continuity? The 1989 National Survey of American Jews* [New York: American Jewish Committee, 1991], p. 59).

19. Richard L. Zweigenhaft and G. William Domhoff, in *Jews in the Protestant Establishment* (New York: Praeger, 1982), credit the term "J.A.S.P." to Peter I. Rose (p. 107). See also Robert C. Christopher, *Crashing the Gates: The De-WASPing of America's Power Elite* (New York: Simon & Schuster, 1989), pp. 43–44.

20. See Charles Silberman, *A Certain People: American Jews and Their Lives Today* (New York: Summit Books, 1985), p. 145. Silberman has updated the statistics originally presented in Harriet Zuckerman, *Scientific Elite: Nobel Laureates in the United States* (New York: Columbia University Press, 1977), p. 68.

21. David Brion Davis, review of Edward S. Shapiro, *The Jewish People in America*, vol. 5: *A Time for Healing: American Jewry Since World* War *II*, in *New Republic*, April 12, 1993. (Shapiro summarized several sociological surveys.) Moreover, the 1986 edition of the *World Almanac and Book of Facts* ranked eight Jewish women, whose occupations range from historian to syndicated columnist to women's rights leader to novelist, as among "America's 25 Most Influential Women"—fully 32 percent of the total. Cited in Jacob Rader Marcus, ed., *The Jew in the American World: A Source Book* (Detroit: Wayne State University Press, 1996), p. 519.

22. Depending on the year, somewhere between 25 and 40 percent of the students at Ivy League schools are Jewish (Norman F. Cantor, *The Sacred Chain: The History of the Jews* [New York: HarperCollins, 1994], p. 400). If we use a low figure of 30 percent, and then take a high estimate of Jews as 2.5 percent of the general U.S. population, we can calculate the rate of disproportional Jewish representation in the Ivies as twelve times greater than Jewish presence in the overall population.

23. Lipset and Raab, p. 75. The poll was conducted in 1985. As of 1996, both of California's U.S. senators are Jewish, as are eight other members of Congress from the state.

24. Goldberg, p. 6.

25. Ibid.

26. Quoted in Goldberg, p. 147.

27. Quoted in Rodger Kamenetz, *The Jew in the Lotus* (San Francisco: HarperSan Francisco, 1994), p. 48.

28. Ibid.

Organizations to Contact

The editors have compiled the following list of organizations concerned with the issues debated in this book. The descriptions are derived from materials provided by the organizations. All have publications or information available for interested readers. The list was compiled on the date of publication of the present volume; the information provided here may change. Be aware that many organizations take several weeks or longer to respond to inquiries, so allow as much time as possible.

American-Israeli Cooperative Enterprise (AICE)
2810 Blaine Dr., Chevy Chase, MD 20815
(301) 565-3918 • fax: (301) 587-9056
e-mail: mgbard@aol.com • website: http://www.us-israel.org

AICE seeks to strengthen the U.S.-Israel relationship by emphasizing values the two nations have in common and developing cooperative social and educational programs that address shared domestic problems. It also works to enhance Israel's image by publicizing novel Israeli solutions to these problems. It publishes the book *Partners for Change: How U.S.-Israel Cooperation Can Benefit America,* and its website contains resources on responding to anti-Semitism.

American Jewish Committee (AJC)
Jacob Blaustein Building, 165 E. 56 St., New York, NY 10022
(212) 751-4000
website: http://ajc.org

AJC works to strengthen U.S.-Israel relations, build international support for Israel, and support the Israeli-Arab peace process. The committee's numerous publications include the *AJC Journal,* the report *Bigotry on Campus: A Planned Response,* the paper "Anti-Semitism in Contemporary America," and the book *Approaches to Antisemitism: Context and Curriculum.*

Anti-Defamation League (ADL)
823 United Nations Plaza, New York, NY 10017
(212) 490-2525
website: http://www.adl.org

The Anti-Defamation League's mission is "to stop the defamation of the Jewish people . . . to secure justice and fair treatment to all citizens alike." An international human relations/civil rights agency, ADL works through education, legislation, litigation, communication, and persuasion to counteract all forms of anti-Semitism, racism, and intolerance; investigate and expose extremists, bigots, and hate movements; build understanding among racial, religious, and ethnic groups; combat discrimination; and to develop diversity education and training to reduce prejudice. ADL model legislation on hate crimes has been adopted or adapted into law in more than forty states. Its many publications include the reports *1998 Hate Crimes Laws* and *Schooled in Hate: Anti-Semitism on Campus.*

B'nai B'rith

1640 Rhode Island Ave. NW, Washington, DC 20036-3278
e-mail: internet@bnaibrith.org • website: http://bnaibrith.org

B'nai B'rith is a network of members in fifty-five nations around the world who work to protect the rights of Jews. It maintains a full-time presence in the United Nations and in Israel, and it raises awareness about anti-Semitism through the Anti-Defamation League, a program of B'nai B'rith. It publishes the magazine *Jewish Monthly* as well as reports and analyses of anti-Semitic terrorism.

Committee for Accuracy in Middle East Reporting in America (CAMERA)

PO Box 428, Boston, MA 02258
(617) 789-3672 • fax: (617) 787-7853
e-mail: media@camera.org • website: http://www.camera.org

CAMERA is a nonprofit media-watch organization dedicated to promoting balanced and accurate coverage of Israel and the Middle East. Through direct responses to student inquiries and its publication *CAMERA on Campus*, it seeks to educate students about Israel, key Middle East issues, and how to respond effectively to anti-Jewish and anti-Israel incidents.

International Fellowship of Christians and Jews (IFCJ)

309 W. Washington, Suite 800, Chicago, IL 60606
(312) 641-7200 • fax: (312) 641-7201
e-mail: info@ifcj.org • website: http://www.ifcj.org

The fellowship works to promote greater understanding between Christians and Jews and to build support for Israel. IFCJ publishes press releases and editorials on several topics, including the religious persecution of Jews and Christians. The Center for Jewish and Christian Values, a program of IFCJ, brings together Jews and Christians in support of a common set of principles on which to improve the moral climate of America.

Jewish Defense League (JDL)

PO Box 480370, Los Angeles, CA 90048
(818) 980-8535
e-mail: jdljdl@aol.com • website: http://www.jdl.org

The league is an activist organization that works to raise awareness of anti-Semitism and the neo-Nazi movement. Its members disagree with the opinion that Jews should not make waves or fight back when they are under attack. The JDL website features news and updates on hate groups and activism as well as information on Jewish culture.

Simon Wiesenthal Center

9760 W. Pico Blvd., Los Angeles, CA 90035
(310) 553-9036 • fax: (310) 553-8007
e-mail: webmaster@wiesenthal.com • website: http://www.wiesenthal.com

The center works to fight anti-Semitism and bigotry around the world. It publishes the quarterly magazine *Response* and maintains a resource center of materials on the Holocaust, twentieth-century genocides, anti-Semitism, racism, and related issues, which it makes available to students.

Vidal Sassoon International Center for the Study of Antisemitism
Hebrew University of Jerusalem, Mount Scopus Campus
Jerusalem 91905, ISRAEL
Tel: 972-2-5882494 • Fax: 972-2-5881002
e-mail: mshelene@mscc.huji.ac.il • website: http://sicsa.huji.ac.il/

The center is an interdisciplinary research center dedicated to understanding anti-Semitism. The center engages in research on anti-Semitism, focusing on relations between Jews and non-Jews in situations of tension and crisis. It publishes the newsletter *SICSA Report*, an annual report, and papers in the Analysis of Current Trends in Antisemitism series and the Studies in Anti-semitism series.

Bibliography

Books

Elliott Abrams	*Faith or Fear: How Jews Can Survive in a Christian America.* New York: Free Press, 1997.
Paul Berman, ed.	*Blacks and Jews: Alliances and Arguments.* New York: Delacorte Press, 1994.
Werner Cohn	*Partners in Hate: Noam Chomsky and the Holocaust Deniers.* Cambridge, MA: Avukah Press, 1995.
Alan M. Dershowitz	*The Vanishing American Jew: In Search of Jewish Identity for the Next Century.* New York: Little, Brown, 1997.
Leonard Dinnerstein	*Antisemitism in America.* New York: Oxford University Press, 1994.
Deborah Dwork and Robert Jan van Pelt	*Auschwitz: 1270 to the Present.* New York: W.W. Norton, 1996.
Murray Friedman	*What Went Wrong?: The Creation and Collapse of the Black-Jewish Alliance.* New York: Free Press, 1995.
John George and Laird M. Wilcox	*American Extremists: Militias, Supremacists, Klansmen, Communist & Others.* Amherst, NY: Prometheus, 1996.
J.J. Goldberg	*Jewish Power: Inside the American Jewish Establishment.* Reading, MA: Addison-Wesley, 1996.
Daniel Jonah Goldhagen	*Hitler's Willing Executioners: Ordinary Germans and the Holocaust.* New York: Knopf, 1996.
David G. Goodman and Masanori Miyazawa	*Jews in the Japanese Mind: The History and Uses of a Cultural Stereotype.* New York: Free Press, 1995.
Frederic Cople Jaher	*A Scapegoat in the New Wilderness: The Origins and Rise of Anti-Semitism in America.* Cambridge, MA: Harvard University Press, 1994.
Paul Kuttner	*The Holocaust: Hoax or History?: The Book of Answers to Those Who Would Deny the Holocaust.* New York: Dawnwood Press, 1996.
Philip Lamy	*Millennium Rage: Survivalists, White Supremacists, and the Doomsday Prophecy.* New York: Plenum Press, 1996.
Albert S. Lindemann	*Esau's Tears: Modern Anti-Semitism and the Rise of the Jews.* New York: Cambridge University Press, 1997.
John J. Michalczyk, ed.	*Resisters, Rescuers, and Refugees: Historical and Ethical Issues.* Kansas City, MO: Sheed & Ward, 1997.

Michael Phayer and Eva Fleischner — *Cries in the Night: Women Who Challenged the Holocaust.* Kansas City, MO: Sheed & Ward, 1997.

James Ridgeway — *Blood in the Face: The Ku Klux Klan, Aryan Nations, Nazi Skinheads, and the Rise of a New White Culture.* New York: Thunder's Mouth Press, 1995.

Periodicals

Edward Alexander — "Multiculturalists and Anti-Semitism," *Society*, September/October 1994.

Zygmunt Bauman — "Hereditary Victimhood: The Holocaust's Life as a Ghost," *Tikkun*, July/August 1998.

William F. Buckley Jr. — "God and Man at Dartmouth," *New York Times*, November 18, 1997.

William F. Buckley Jr. — "Jews and Christians Have Equivalent Duties," *Conservative Chronicle*, May 3, 1995. Available from P.O. Box 29, Hampton, IA 50441.

Edward Conlon — "The Uses of Malice: Jews in the Slave Trade, and Other Myths," *American Spectator*, April 1995.

Marc Cooper — "The Paranoid Style," *Nation*, April 10, 1995.

Tyler Cowen — "The Socialist Roots of Modern Anti-Semitism," *Freeman*, January 1997. Available from The Foundation for Economic Education, Irvington-on-Hudson, NY 10533.

Midge Decter — "A Jew in Anti-Christian America," *First Things*, October 1995. Available from 156 Fifth Ave., Suite 400, New York, NY 10010.

Katherine Dwyer — "France's New Nazis: The Resistible Rise of Jean-Marie LePen," *International Socialist Review*, Fall 1997. Available from P.O. Box 258082, Chicago, IL 60625.

Christopher John Farley — "Enforcing Correctness," *Time*, February 7, 1994.

Jonathan Kaufman — "Some Liberal Jews, to Their Own Surprise, See a Rise in Bigotry," *Wall Street Journal*, March 8, 1995.

David Klinghoffer — "Anti-Semitism Without Anti-Semites," *First Things*, April 1998.

Daniel Levitas — "Sleeping with the Enemy: A.D.L. and the Christian Right," *Nation*, June 19, 1995.

Andrew Nagorski — "A Strange Affair," *Newsweek*, June 15, 1998.

Norman Podhoretz — "In the Matter of Pat Robertson," *Commentary*, August 1995.

Ephraim Radner — "New World Order, Old World Anti-Semitism," *Christian Century*, September 13–20, 1995.

Ruth Rosen — "Blacks and Jews' Documentary Puts Tensions into Historical Context," *Liberal Opinion Week*, August 11, 1997. Available from P.O. Box 880, Vinton, IA 52349.

Paul Shore   "Farrakhan and the Filling of the Mythic Gap,"
                       Humanist, July/August 1994.

Joseph Sobran   "The Jewish Establishment," *Sobran's*, September 1995.
                       Available from P.O. Box 1383, Vienna, VA 22183.

Alessandra Stanley   "Success May Be Bad for Jews as Old Russian Bias Sur-
                       faces," *New York Times*, April 15, 1997.

Ruth R. Wisse   "The National Prospect," *Commentary*, November 1995.

Don Wycliff   "Why Farrakhan Appeals: Touching the Souls of Black
                       Folk," *Commonweal*, November 17, 1995.

Stephen Zunes   "Anti-Semitism in U.S. Middle East Policy," *Z Magazine*,
                       March 1995.

Index